Spelling Rules!

Janelle Ho and
Helen Pearson

NSW Edition

Name: ________________________________

Class: ________________________________

Contents

SLLURP

SLLURP summarises the spelling strategies that you can use to learn new words.

Say	Say the word carefully and slowly to yourself.
Listen	Listen to how each part of the word sounds in sequence.
Look	Look at the patterns of letters in the word and the shape of the word.
Understand	Understand rules, word meanings and word origins.
Remember	Remember all the similar words you can already spell and relate this knowledge to any new word.
Practise	Practise writing the word until it is firmly fixed in your long-term memory.

Scope and Sequence

This scope and sequence chart is based on the requirements of the NSW Curriculum.

Unit	Skill focus				Other	Word list
	Vowels	Consonants	Letter patterns	Rules and tips		
1	short sounds	digraphs		add 's', 'ed', 'ing'		hip, hop, ship, shop, dish, fill, shell, pack, wish, luck
2		initial 2-consonant blends		impossible combinations (e.g. tl)		clap, crab, flag, glad, plot, stop, skin, trip, crack, smell
3		final 2-consonant blends			CCVCC words	fast, chest, desk, wasp, hint, grunt, stamp, spilt, crust, grand
4	a, a-e, ea			drop silent 'e' to add suffix	break/brake, steak/stake, great/grate	baby, potato, save, face, blame, shame, stale, break, great, steak
5	ai		ay		sail/sale, plain/plane	brain, plain, chain, sail, trail, again, pay, stay, sway, away
6			ey, eigh		ate/eight, prey/pray	they, grey, prey, obey, eight, weigh, weight, sleigh, neigh, neighbour
7	REVISION					
8		ll, ff, ss, zz		comparative -er and -est	Double letters do not start a word.	tall, small, dull, stiff, cliff, stuff, bluff, grass, dress, buzz
9	e, e-e, ee, ea				been/bean, week/weak, leek/leak, steel/steal	equal, even, week, keep, sleep, east, steal, speak, dream, cheat
10	ie		ey		piece/peace	chief, thief, field, shield, piece, believe, key, honey, monkey, turkey
11	short y			suffix 'y': double final consonant		jelly, silly, happy, body, puppy, funny, sunny, bumpy, sleepy, wobbly
12	i, i-e, long y			change 'y' to 'i' to add suffix		kind, lion, tiger, behind, five, nine, glide, try, spy, reply
13	ie		igh		silent letter: kn know, knee, knight	pie, lie, tie, sigh, high, thigh, right, night, bright, flight
14	REVISION					
15	o, o-e			drop silent 'e' to add suffix		most, post, piano, radio, hope, rose, joke, woke, broke, quote
16	oa		ow			coat, goat, soap, loaf, float, toast, show, flow, know, yellow
17		ch, sh		add 'es' to to words that end in 'ch' or 'sh'		beach, teach, speech, bunch, lunch, flash, crash, crush, blush, swish
18	ou		ow			shout, about, around, house, pounce, town, crowd, brown, flower, allow
19	oi		oy			toy, enjoy, annoy, loyal, coin, noise, oil, spoil, point, toilet
20		wh			were/we're/where	who, why, when, where, what, which, wheel, whale, white, wheat
21	REVISION					
22		initial 3-consonant blends		double final consonant to add suffix	CCCVC and CCCVCC words	splash, split, spray, sprain, sprint, street, stripe, screen, scream, scrub
23		thr, shr				three, throat, thread, throw, throne, thrill, shrill, shrub, shrug, shriek
24		ng, nk			irregular verbs: sing/sang, sink/sank, spring/sprang, shrink/shrank	fling, spring, angry, hungry, finger, sink, plank, shrink, ankle, blanket
25	long oo				compound words with 'room'	boo, roof, cool, smooth, choose, balloon, cartoon, bedroom, bathroom, boomerang
26			ew		irregular verbs: draw/drew, know/knew, grow/grew, throw/threw	new, few, dew, news, knew, drew, threw, screw, jewel, view
27	u-e, ue			drop silent 'e' to add suffix		cute, tune, tube, refuse, true, glue, clue, argue, value, rescue
28	REVISION					
29					numbers 1–10 one/won, to/two/too, four/for, eight/ate	one, two, three, four, five, six, seven, eight, nine, ten
30	u, short oo					bull, pull, push, put, sugar, look, cook, wood, stood, shook
31		ld	oul		wood/would	held, bald, hold, scold, world, build, could, would, should, shoulder
32					compound words	sunhat, gumboot, bedside, shoelace, toenail, jellyfish, earring, hairbrush, newspaper, wheelchair
33			er		family words	mother, father, sister, brother, grandmother, grandfather, elder, aunt, uncle, family
34			er, or	suffixes -er, -or for people		baker, writer, driver, swimmer, manager, builder, actor, doctor, sailor, author
35	REVISION					

Note to Teachers and Parents

Spelling Rules!

Some students are natural spellers. But the vast majority of students need formal, systematic and sequential instruction about the way spelling works and the strategies they can use to become independent, confident spellers.

The *Spelling Rules!* program is based on sound linguistic and pedagogical theory. It is informed by research into how students of different ages acquire and apply spelling skills, and how those skills move from the working to the long-term memory. The program closely follows the NSW English Curriculum. NSW Curriculum references are provided in the two Teacher Resource Books. The program consists of seven Student Books.

Each student book contains units of work, with each unit designed to be used over the course of a week. The content of each unit follows the suggested instructional sequence in the NSW English syllabus. Each unit simultaneously develops new skills and reinforces skills from previous units. Where appropriate, topic words from other curriculum areas are included. When spelling rules and tips are introduced, only known sounds and letter patterns are used so that students focus on one skill at a time. Regular revision units enable teachers to assess student progress and reinforce key rules and patterns from previous units. Books 1 to 6 also include a simple reflection activity that encourages students to assess their own progress and provides you with a starting point for discussion.

Spelling knowledge

Learning to spell involves developing different kinds of spelling knowledge:

- **Kinaesthetic knowledge** – the physical feeling when saying different sounds and words, and when writing the shapes of letters and words
- **Phonological knowledge** – how a word sounds and the patterns of sounds in words
- **Visual knowledge** – how letters and words look and the visual patterns in words
- **Morphemic knowledge** – the meaning or function of words or parts of words
- **Etymological knowledge** – the origins and history of words and the effect this has on spelling patterns.

Icons used in Student Book 1

The following icons identify the main spelling strategy that students will use to complete an activity.

Say the word. (Kinaesthetic knowledge) These activities ask students to experience how sounds feel in the mouth and jaw. Changing the positions of the jaw, lips, and tongue changes the sounds we make. Encourage students to pronounce the sounds and words accurately. If they mispronounce a sound or word, they may misrepresent it in writing.

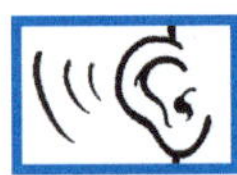

Listen to the word. (Phonological knowledge) These activities focus on discriminating between different sounds and breaking up words into syllables or individual sound segments (phonemes).

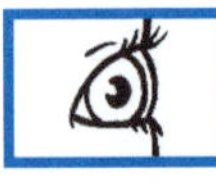

Look at the word. (Visual knowledge) These activities help students to see how the sound is represented using combinations of letters, and to associate this visual pattern with what they are hearing. Students will develop the ability to know when a word does or does not 'look right'.

Understand the word. (Morphemic and etymological knowledge) These activities focus on word meanings, word families, prefixes and suffixes, spelling rules, word origins and so on – all of which help embed spelling in the long-term memory.

Practise writing the word. (Kinaesthetic knowledge) These activities develop students' awareness of the physical movement involved in writing the word. By practising writing the word a number of times and in different contexts, the spelling becomes embedded in the long-term memory.

This icon highlights useful spelling rules.

This icon tells students that a special clue or hint is provided for an activity. It may be a spelling, grammar or punctuation convention, or a definition of a useful term.

Encourages students to assess their progress through each unit.

Spelling Rules! Student Book 1 (ISBN 9780655092582) © Janelle Ho, Helen Pearson/Matilda Education Australia

Student Book 1

Units of work

Student Book 1 contains 35 weekly units of work. Groups of units focus on different phonemes that represent the same sound. The suffixes taught in Book K are consolidated using new words. They are also elaborated on by using spelling rules such as the dropping of silent 'e' and the doubling of the final consonant. More suffixes (*y*, *es*, *er* and *or*) are taught and homophones are explained and practised. Finally, the concepts of irregular verbs and compound words are also presented. See the **Scope and Sequence** chart on page 3 for more information.

Word lists

In *Student Book 1*, each unit (except Revision units) has a list of ten spelling words. The words are selected to support the learning focus and spelling strategies in the unit. The list also includes words from other curriculum areas such as mathematics, science and social sciences. Where appropriate, Aboriginal Australian English words are also included.

SLLURP

Each word list begins with a reminder for students to SLLURP. SLLURP summarises the strategies that will help spelling move from students' working memory to their long-term memory. These strategies are provided on page 2, for easy reference.

Unit at a glance

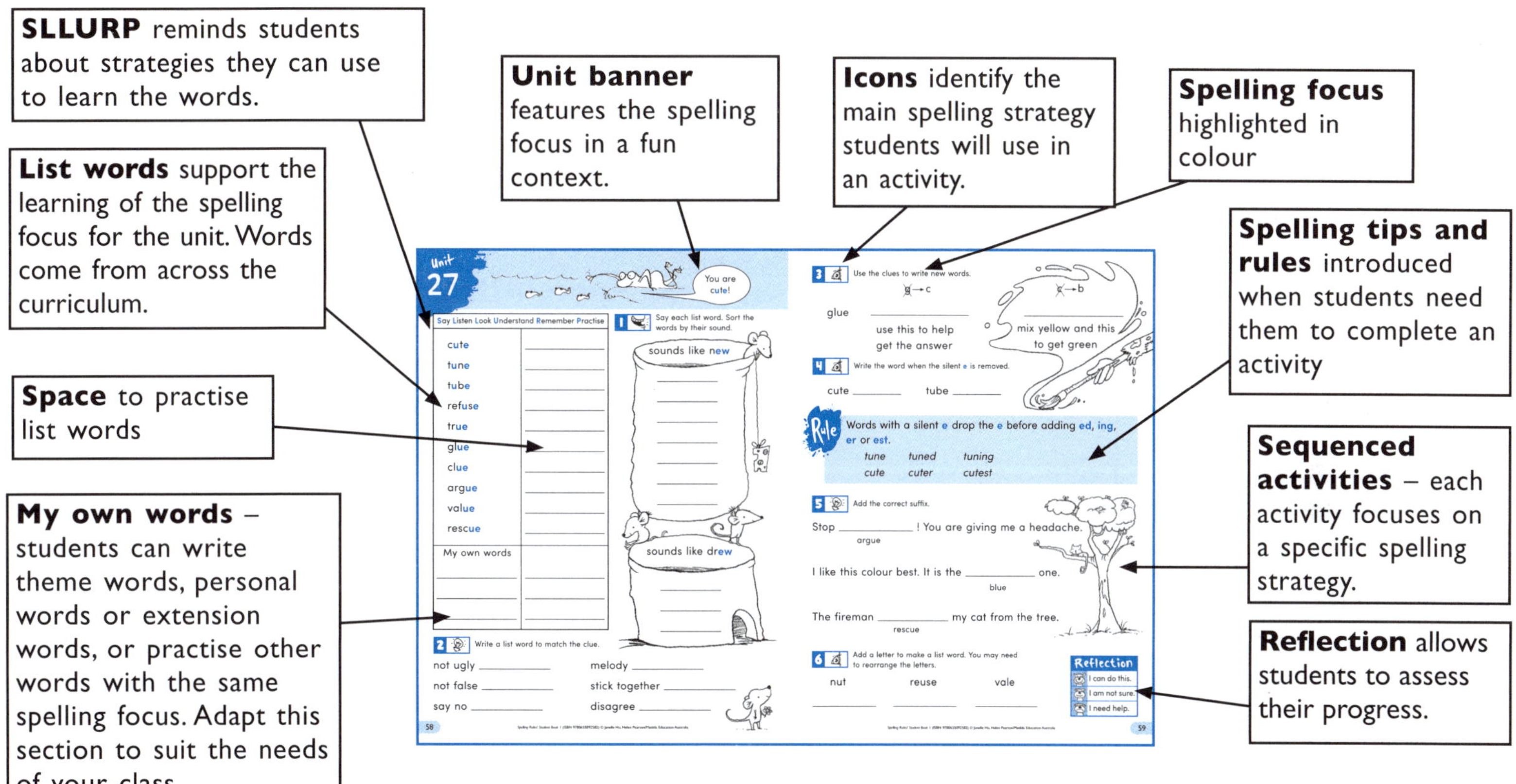

Spelling Rules! Teacher Resource Book K–2

Full teacher support for *Student Book 1* is provided by *Spelling Rules! Teacher Resource Book K–2*. Here you will find valuable background information about spelling development and spelling knowledge, along with practical resources, such as:

- teaching tips for every unit in *Student Book 1*
- extra word lists
- strategies for teaching spelling
- guidelines for assessing spelling and diagnosing spelling errors
- activities to support struggling spellers
- worthwhile extension for more able spellers.

Unit 1

Say Listen Look Understand Remember Practise	
hip	________
hop	________
ship	________
shop	________
dish	________
fill	________
shell	________
pack	________
wish	________
luck	________
My own words	
________	________
________	________
________	________

1 Write a list word that has the small word in it.

hip ________

hop ________

is ________

ill ________

he ________

2 Write a list word that rhymes.

top ________

bell ________

back ________

fish ________

3 Write list words.

I will _ i _ _ this bag with rocks.

Look at the big _ _ e _ _ I found.

You can _ a _ _ your books in this box.

Spelling Rules! Student Book 1 (ISBN 9780655092582) © Janelle Ho, Helen Pearson/Matilda Education Australia

Write the words. Choose one to finish the sentence.

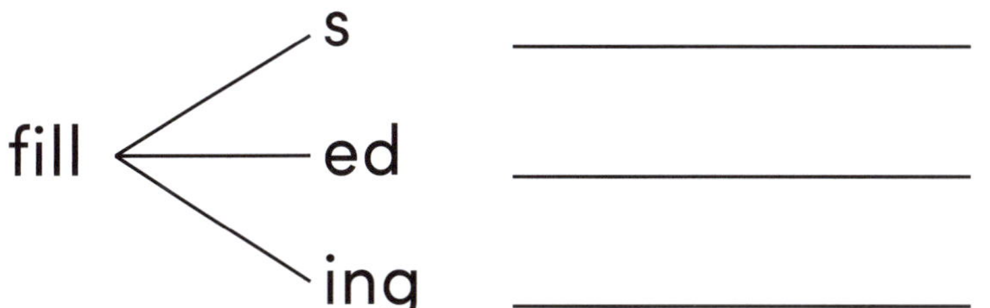

Mum is ______________ the box with grapes.

John ______________ his own lunch box last week.

5 Write **a**, **e**, **i**, **o** or **u**.

n__ck t__ck d__ck s__ck s__ck

Write the plural word.

Say both words. Colour the correct one.

Ducks | quack | quick | when they want food.

Shut your eyes and make a | wash | wish |.

Jack and Jill | fill | fell | down the hill.

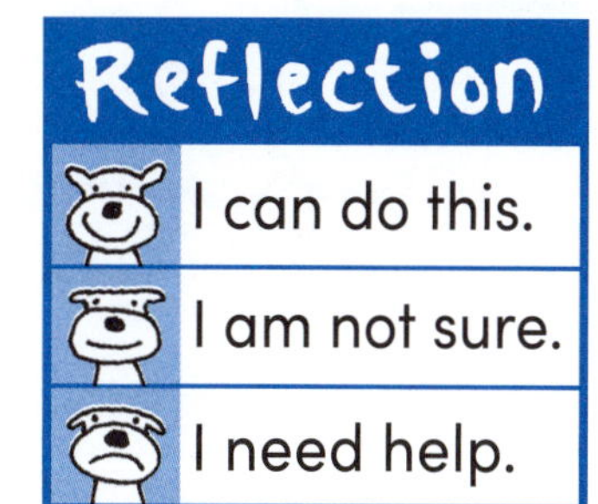

Unit 2

Slap on a hat when the sun is hot!

Say Listen Look Understand Remember Practise	
clap	___
crab	___
flag	___
glad	___
plot	___
stop	___
skin	___
trip	___
crack	___
smell	___
My own words	
___	___
___	___
___	___

1 Write list words.

2 Write list words.

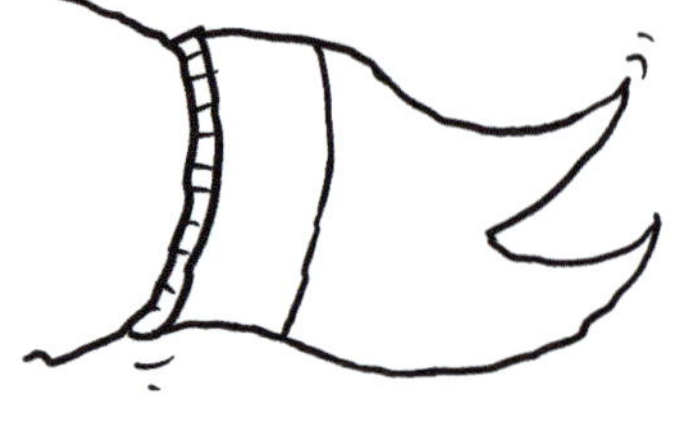

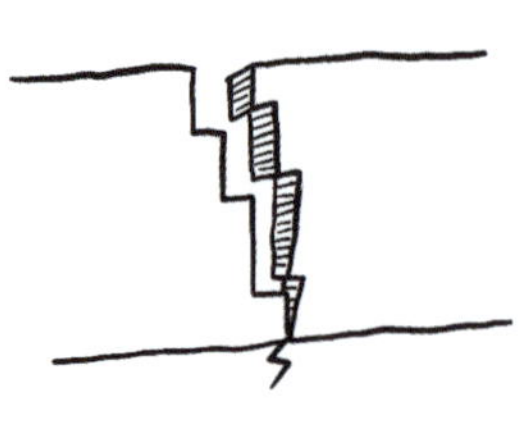

___ ___ ___ ___

3 Look for a small word in the list word. Write the small word.

stop ____________ trip ____________ glad ____________

skin ____________ plot ____________ crack ____________

Some letters do not go together at the beginning of a word.

4 Rearrange the letters to make a word. Start with two consonants.

lpan ____________ tsem ____________ rgab ____________

ltils ____________ rtap ____________ ccolk ____________

5 Make words with these letters.

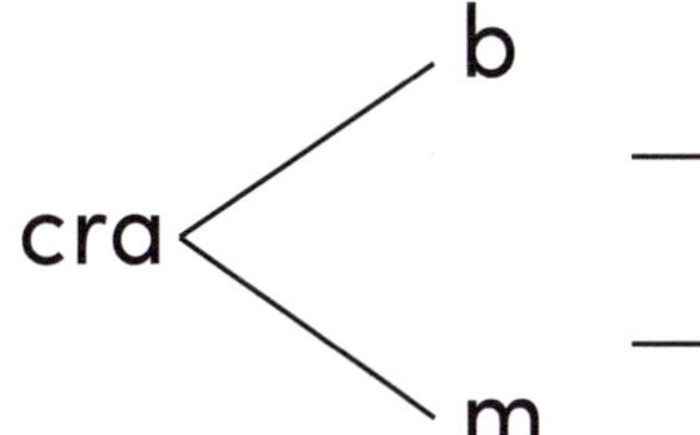

____

____

____

____

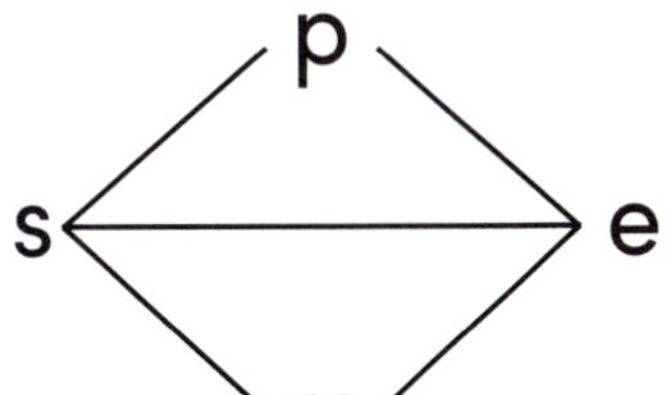

____

____

____

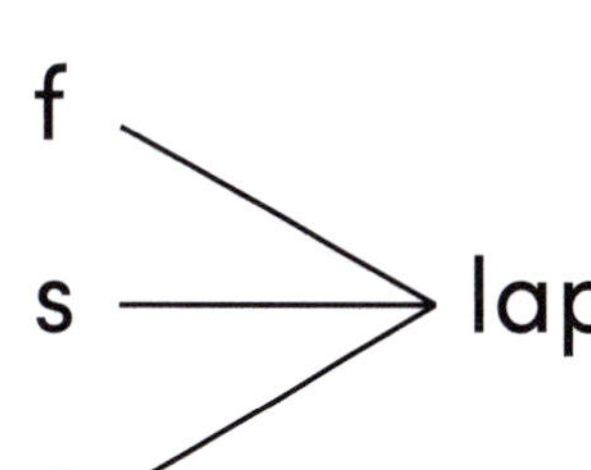

____

____

____

6 Write list words to complete the sentences.

Your ____________ feels hot. You must be sunburnt.

I am so ____________ you are feeling better.

Jan's family went on a road ____________ during the summer.

Unit 3

Say Listen Look Understand Remember Practise	
fast	______
chest	______
desk	______
wasp	______
hint	______
grunt	______
stamp	______
spilt	______
crust	______
grand	______
My own words	
______	______
______	______
______	______

1 Say each word. Sort the box words by their vowel sound.

fast   wasp   stamp   grand

a as in cat

______

______

a as in ball

______

a as in pass

______

2 Change the underlined letter to make a list word.

h<u>u</u>nt ______

<u>p</u>ast ______

w<u>i</u>sp ______

3 Write a list word.

______   ______   ______   ______

Spelling Rules! Student Book 1 (ISBN 9780655092582) © Janelle Ho, Helen Pearson/Matilda Education Australia

4 Draw a line between each sound. The first one has been done for you.

f / a / s / t   c h e s t   d e s k   w a s p   h i n t

g r u n t   s t a m p   s p i l t   c r u s t   g r a n d

5 Write a sentence to describe each picture. Use a list word in each sentence.

____

____

____

____

____

____

6 Write **ed** or **ing** to finish each sentence.

Stan stamp______ his feet to get rid of the sand.

Emma is hint______ to her mother that she wants to go home.

The pig grunt______ to show that it was full.

Every day during Ramadan, Muslims finish fast______ at sunset.

7 Some letters do not go together.
Circle the words that cannot be found in English.

trash   srill   brick

tsem   cling   lramp

Spelling Rules! Student Book 1 (ISBN 9780655092582)

Unit 4

Don't forget the baby!

Say Listen Look Understand Remember Practise	
baby	______
potato	______
save	______
face	______
blame	______
shame	______
stale	______
break	______
great	______
steak	______
My own words	
______	______
______	______
______	______

1 Write list words.

______

______

______

______

2 Write a list word that has the small word in it.

ham ______

beak ______

pot ______

lame ______

tale ______

3 Write a list word that rhymes.

brave	fail	shake	ate
______	______	______	______

Spelling Rules! Student Book 1 (ISBN 9780655092582) © Janelle Ho, Helen Pearson/Matilda Education Australia

Two words that sound the same but are not spelt the same are called **homophones**.

break brake *steak stake* *great grate*

4 Write the correct homophone.

The left ____________ on your bike is not working.

Dad prefers kebabs to ____________.

I hope to go see the ____________ Barrier Reef one day.

Rule

Words with a silent **e** drop the **e** before adding **ed** or **ing**.

name → named *name → naming*

like → liked *like → liking*

5 Write the word when you add **ed** and **ing**.

save	________	________	hope	________	________
face	________	________	time	________	________
blame	________	________	smile	________	________
shame	________	________	toe	________	________

6 Colour the correct word.

Paul drew a poster that said, " Safe | Save the koalas!"

The robber tried to steal | stale the car.

Unit 5

Don't stay away all day!

Say Listen Look Understand Remember Practise	
brain	
plain	
chain	
sail	
trail	
again	
pay	
stay	
sway	
away	
My own words	

1 Make **ai** words.

s fr r t p tr j ail

m p br pl ch tr g ain

2 Draw shapes to match the **ay** words. Circle the words that have the same shape.

pay stay away sway

Spelling Rules! Student Book 1 (ISBN 9780655092582)

ay sounds the same as **ai**.

A syllable with **ai** must always end with a consonant.

say sail *ray rain*

3 Fill in **ay** or **ai** to show the vowel sound.

p__ __ r__ __ st__ __ pl__ __ p__ __d

r__ __d st__ __n pl__ __n p__ __n r__ __n

These words are **homophones**.

sail sale *plain plane*

4 Write the correct homophone.

sail sale	Let's ____________ to the island. The red car is for ____________.
plain plane	Did you see the ____________ take off? Draw on the ____________ paper.

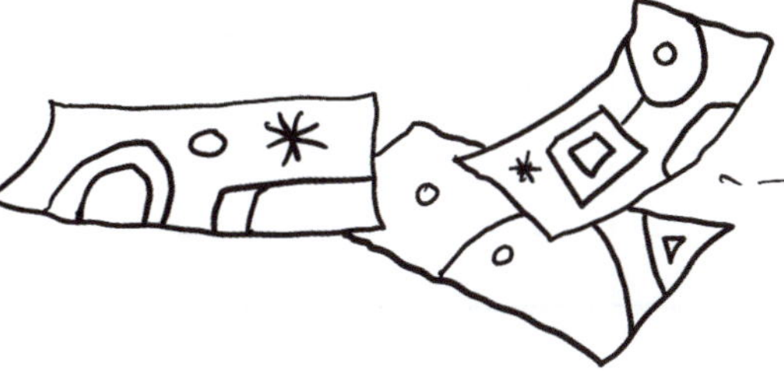

5 Write **ai** or **ay** words to finish the rhyme.

____________, ____________, go ____________!

Come ____________ another day.

Reflection

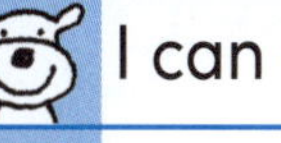

I can do this.

I am not sure.

I need help.

Unit 6

Say Listen Look Understand Remember Practise	
they	___
grey	___
prey	___
obey	___
eight	___
weigh	___
weight	___
sleigh	___
neigh	___
neighbour	___
My own words	
___	___
___	___
___	___

1 Draw a line between each sound.

t h e y
p r e y
e i g h t
w e i g h t
n e i g h

g r e y
o b e y
w e i g h
s l e i g h

2 Write ey or eigh.

th ___ | ___ t
gr ___ | w ___ t
pr ___ | w ___
ob ___ | sl ___
n ___ | n ___ bour

3 Write a list word.

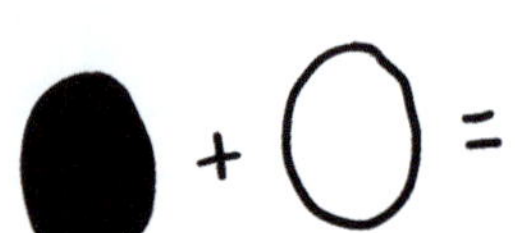

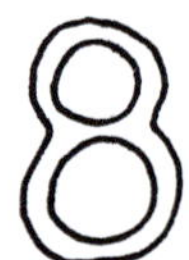

___ ___ ___ ___

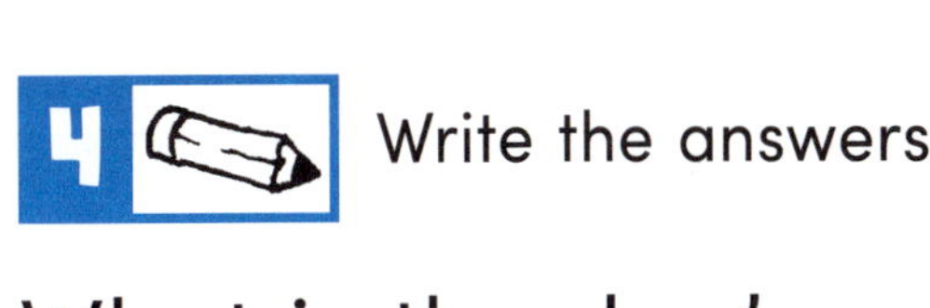

Write the answers.

What is the dog's weight?

The dog's ______________ is 25 kilograms.

How much do you weigh?

I ______________________________.

These words are **homophones**.

ate eight *prey pray*

Colour the correct homophone.

I | ate | eight | my lunch at recess.

Four plus four is | ate | eight |.

Hindus and Buddhists | pray | prey | in a temple.

In the wild, the lion has many | pray | prey |.

Write a list word.

The sound a horse makes ______________

The number after seven ______________

Not we ______________

To do as your parents say ______________

The person who lives next door ______________

What a predator eats ______________

Unit 7 Revision

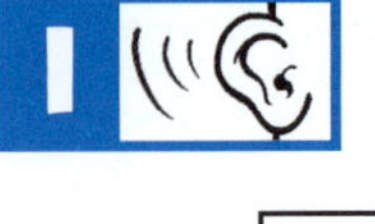

1 Vowels can make different sounds. Sort the words by listening to their sound.

gill	that	weigh	tell	band	sing
pest	name	ate	hen	thin	slap

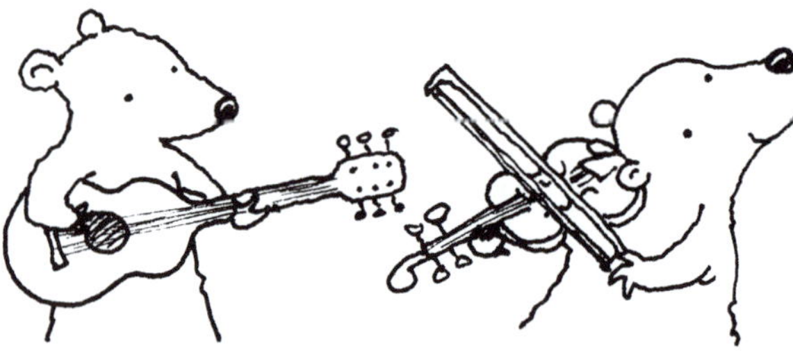

2 Change one letter to make a new word.

shop	wish	lick	ball
______	______	______	______
grey	stay	name	train
______	______	______	______
away	slack	steal	shell
______	______	______	______

3 Label the picture. Use the words in the wall.

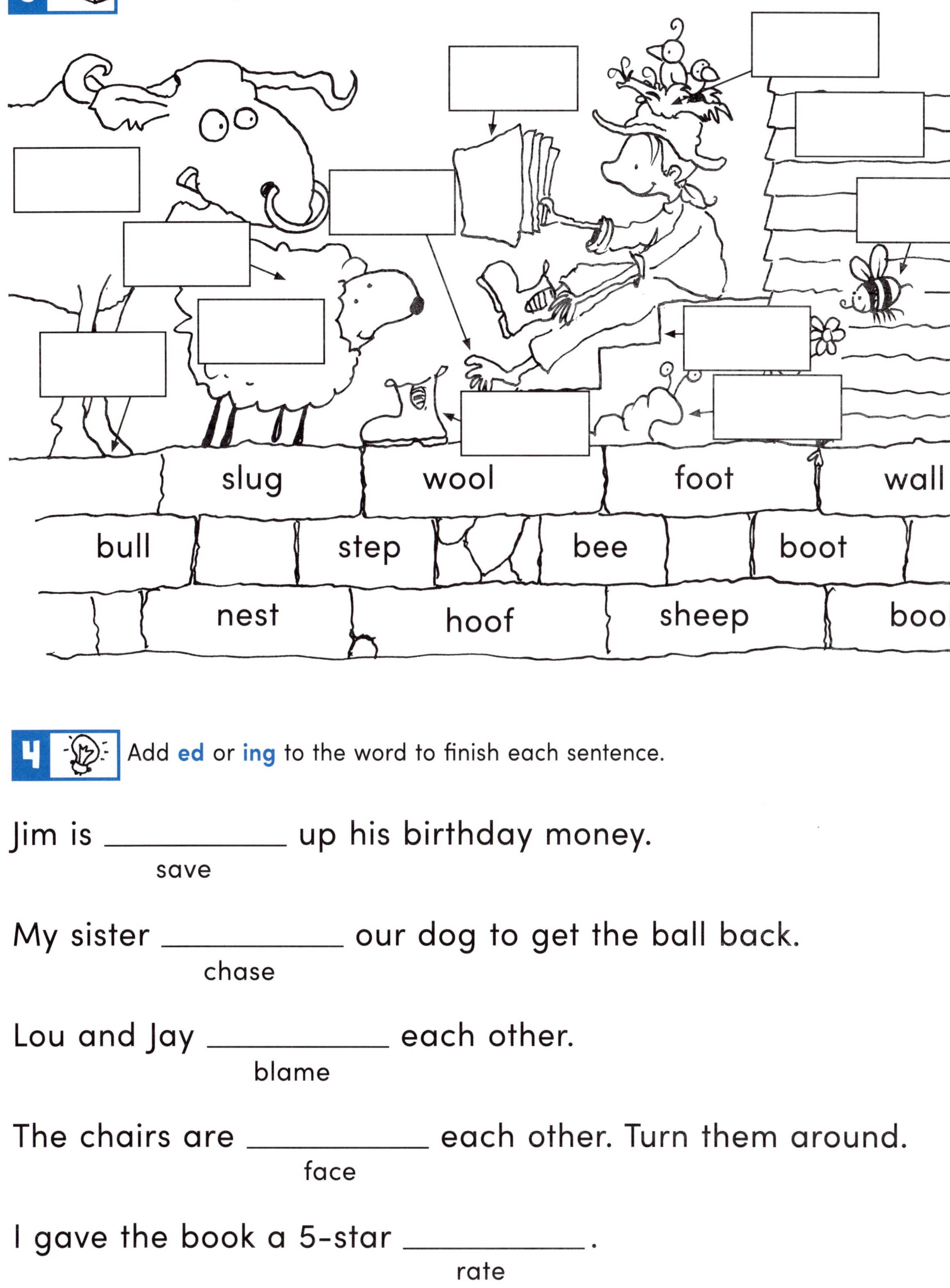

4 Add **ed** or **ing** to the word to finish each sentence.

Jim is __________ up his birthday money.
save

My sister __________ our dog to get the ball back.
chase

Lou and Jay __________ each other.
blame

The chairs are __________ each other. Turn them around.
face

I gave the book a 5-star __________.
rate

Unit 8

Say Listen Look Understand Remember Practise	
tall	
small	
dull	
stiff	
cliff	
stuff	
bluff	
grass	
dress	
buzz	
My own words	

Tip Double letters do not start words.

1 Rearrange the letters to make list words.

llat ________ ffits ________

ssarg ________

llams ________

llud ________

sserd ________

ffuts ________

2 Circle the words that rhyme in the same colour.

fall	chess	small
pull	bluff	dress
mess	dull	puff

Which words are left?

________ ________

3 Use the words to make a wall.

a, all, ball

I, ill, fill

a, all, tall

Spelling Rules! Student Book 1 (ISBN 9780655092582) © Janelle Ho, Helen Pearson/Matilda Education Australia

 Sometimes signs stand for words.

 A heart says love.

 A t__ __ __ says you are right.

 A cr__ __ __ says you are wrong.

 A pl__ __ sign says add together.

 A mi__ __ __ sign says take away.

To compare two things, add **er** to the adjective. *tall* → *taller*
To compare three or more things, add **est**. *tall* → *tallest*

 Add **er** or **est**.

Comparing two things:	tall______	dull______	stiff______
Comparing three things:	tall______	dull______	stiff______

 Colour the correct word.

The | older | oldest | Aboriginal rock art is in Balangarra Country in the Kimberley.

The mouse lemur is | smaller | smallest | than the pygmy rabbit.

Grandad says he feels | stiffer | stiffest | today than yesterday.

What a big dinner! This is the | fuller | fullest | I've ever felt.

 Write a sentence that uses the word **buzz**.

____

____

Reflection
- I can do this.
- I am not sure.
- I need help.

Unit 9

Say Listen Look Understand Remember Practise	
equal	
even	
week	
keep	
sleep	
east	
steal	
speak	
dream	
cheat	
My own words	

1 Write list words.

2 Write the two pairs of list words that rhyme.

3 Write the words.

w / s / l	eek

b / h / ch	eat

k / d / sh	eep

Spelling Rules! Student Book 1 (ISBN 9780655092582)

 Write the new word. Draw a picture to match.

f + east = ______	b + east = ______

These words are **homophones**.

been *bean* *week* *weak*
leek *leak* *steel* *steal*

 Write the correct homophone to complete each sentence.

been bean	Green ______s are yummy! Have you ______ eating them?
week weak	I was away from school last ______. I was feeling ______ from the flu.
leek leak	You can use a ______ in place of an onion. But you can't use it to plug a ______!
steel steal	What did the robber ______? Why did he ______ ______?

Reflection

- I can do this.
- I am not sure.
- I need help.

Spelling Rules! Student Book 1 (ISBN 9780655092582)

Unit 10

Say Listen Look Understand Remember Practise	
chief	________
thief	________
field	________
shield	________
piece	________
believe	________
key	________
honey	________
monkey	________
turkey	________
My own words	
________	________
________	________
________	________

1 Circle the picture if the word has a long **e** sound.

2 Write the missing letters.

p__ __ce

donk__ __

sh__ __d

th__ __f

turk__ __

monk__ __

3 Which **key** words finish these sentences? They are all animals.

We often eat roast ________________ at Christmas.

A ________________ has bigger ears than a horse.

I like to play on the ________________ bars at school.

4 Draw a line between each sound.

key piece chief field

turkey honey believe

These words are **homophones**.

piece peace

5 Colour the correct word.

We all wish for world | piece | peace |.

I also wish for a | piece | peace | of cake!

6 Look for a small word in each list word.
Write the small word.

thief ________ shield ________ piece ________

honey ________ believe ________ ________

7 Colour the correct word.

| Monkey | Monkeys | are some of the cleverest animals in the world.

Some tribes have | chief | chiefs |, but Aboriginal | mob | mobs | have elders.

Dad will meet me at the first | field | fields |.

Mum has five | key | keys | on her key ring.

Unit 11

These are funny words!

Say Listen Look Understand Remember Practise	
jelly	____________
silly	____________
happy	____________
body	____________
puppy	____________
funny	____________
sunny	____________
bumpy	____________
sleepy	____________
wobbly	____________
My own words	
____________	____________
____________	____________
____________	____________

1 Fill in the double letters to make list words.

This je_ _y is very wo_ _ly.

We all like fu_ _y books.

What a sl_ _py pu_ _y!

It will be su_ _y this weekend.

Jonny has a si_ _y hat on.

Let's all try to be ha_ _y today.

2  Colour the box if y has a short sound as in **mummy** or **daddy**.

cry	they	shy
very	dry	dusty
body	sleepy	sticky

Some words add **y** to make an adjective.

Add **y** to make new words.

bump ________ sleep ________

luck ________ mess ________

rock ________ hill ________

If a word has a short vowel sound, double the last letter before adding **y**.

fun → funny *spot → spotty*

Use the rule to make new words.

sun ________ dad ________ chat ________

skin ________ mum ________ flop ________

Write these sentences again with a space between each word.

Mypuppyisverymuddy. ____________________

Isyourtoothwobbly? ____________________

Redjellyissoyummy. ____________________

Read each word. Cross out the word that doesn't belong.

skinny	slim	sticky	thin
shy	muddy	grubby	dusty
funny	jolly	body	witty

Reflection

I can do this.

I am not sure.

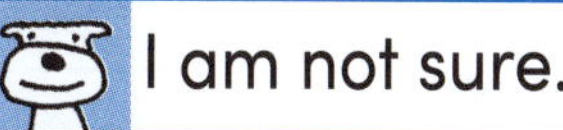

I need help.

Unit 12

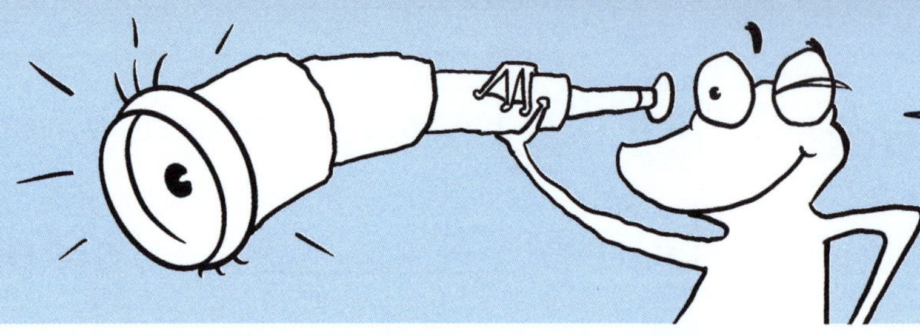

Say Listen Look Understand Remember Practise	
kind	______
lion	______
tiger	______
behind	______
five	______
nine	______
glide	______
try	______
spy	______
reply	______
My own words	
______	______
______	______
______	______

1 Say the words. Write them in the correct space.

chin ride fly

blind stick spider

finger child link

like the **i** in kin

______
______
______
______

like the **i** in kind

______
______
______
______
______

2 Look for small words in each list word.

lion kind behind

______ ______ ______ ______

______ ______ ______ ______

 Write the word in the correct space. Then write two sentences about the picture.

above	behind	below	between

If a word ends in **y**, change **y** to **i** before adding **es** or **ed**.

try ⟶ tries *try ⟶ tried*

 Colour the correct word.

A plane | flyes | flies | over my house every day.

| Dryed | Dried | fruit is not as good as fresh fruit.

The police officer | spyed | spied | the thief in the car.

 Write the list word.

5 ______________ 9 ______________

Reflection

- I can do this.
- I am not sure.
- I need help.

Unit 13

Say Listen Look Understand Remember Practise	
pie	______
lie	______
tie	______
sigh	______
high	______
thigh	______
right	______
night	______
bright	______
flight	______
My own words	
______	______
______	______
______	______

1 Write a list word in each shape.

2 Write a list word.

______ ______ ______ ______

Spelling Rules! Student Book 1 (ISBN 9780655092582) © Janelle Ho, Helen Pearson/Matilda Education Australia

Use the clue to make a new word.

s~~h~~y h→t ________ t~~i~~e i→o ________

f~~l~~ight ________ sigh + t ________

These words are **homophones**. *piece* *peace*
To remember *piece*, think *A piece of pie.*

Write the correct homophone.

This jigsaw puzzle is missing a ____________.

The card said, "Wishing you ____________ and joy."

Some words start with **kn**. *knight* *know* *knee* *kneel*
The letter **k** is silent.

Write the **kn** word.

____

____

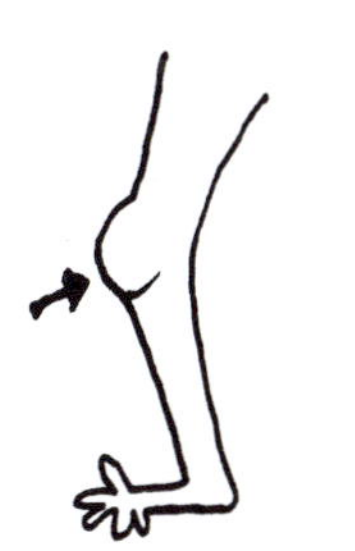

____

____

Spelling Rules! Student Book 1 (ISBN 9780655092582) © Janelle Ho, Helen Pearson/Matilda Education Australia

Say each word. Circle the word in each group that does not rhyme.

spit	weak	field	slid
bite	cheek	child	bride
fight	brake	peeled	cried

Say each word. Sort the words by their vowel sound.

she	chief	blind	creep	cry	slide	tie	east

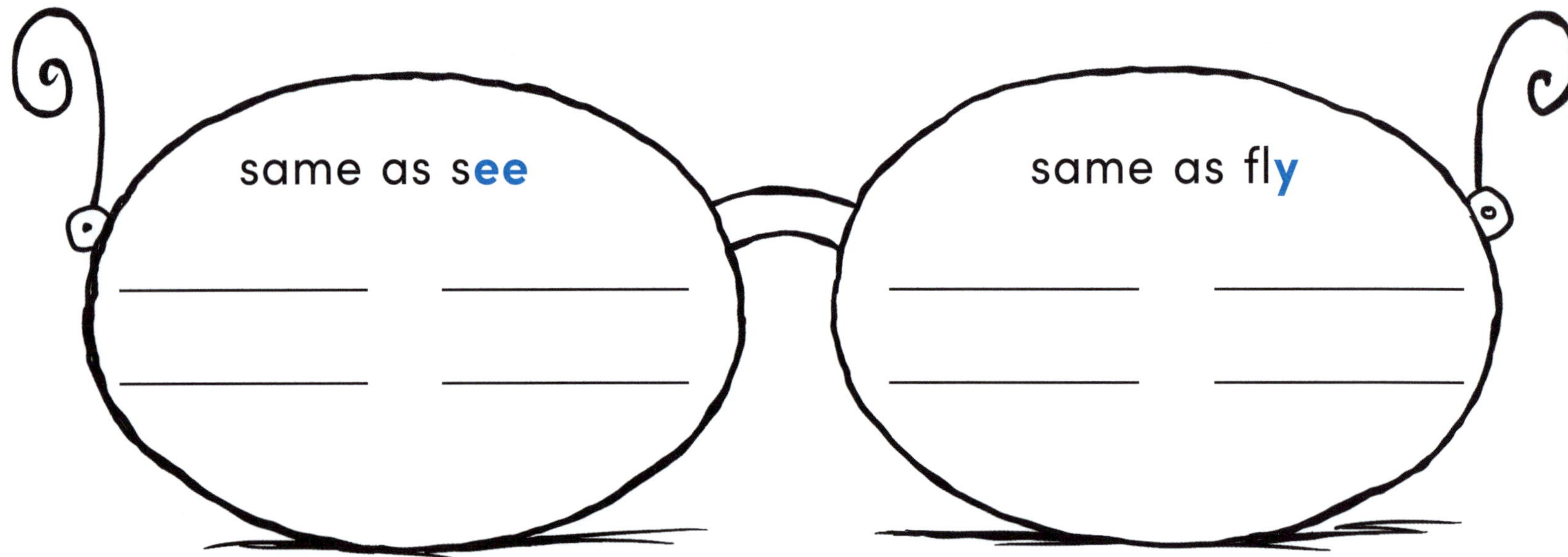

3 Write a list word that is the opposite.

odd ____________ wake ____________ west ____________

strong ____________ dull ____________ day ____________

smooth ____________ wrong ____________ sad ____________

Spelling Rules! Student Book 1 (ISBN 9780655092582) © Janelle Ho, Helen Pearson/Matilda Education Australia

4 Use the clues to write list words. What is the hidden word under the star?

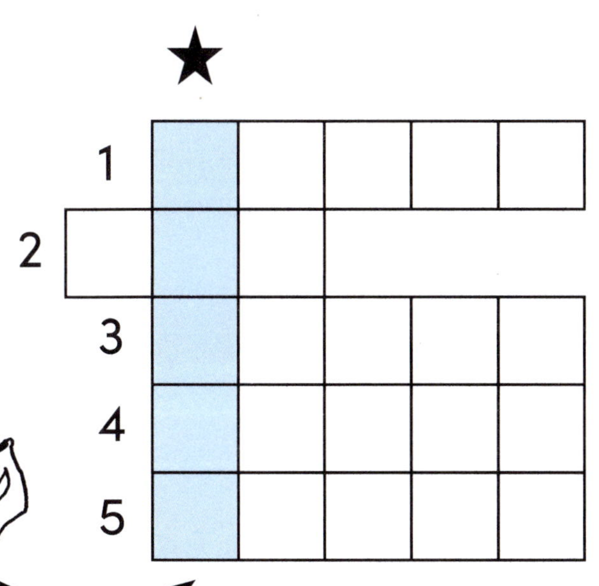

1. 
2. ________ your best!
3. =
4. not big
5. cannot be bent

5 Write the letters to make list words.

ch__ __t	h__g__	sp__	l__on
bel__ __v__	sill__	sl__ __p	f__v__

Remember to change **y** to **i** before adding **er** or **est**.

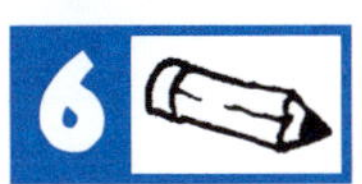

6 Add **er** or **est**.

The sun is the ______________ object in the sky.
bright

Rita is the ______________ person in the class.
funny

Dad looks ______________ than Grandma.
sleepy

Mount Kosciuszko is the ______________ mountain in Australia.
high

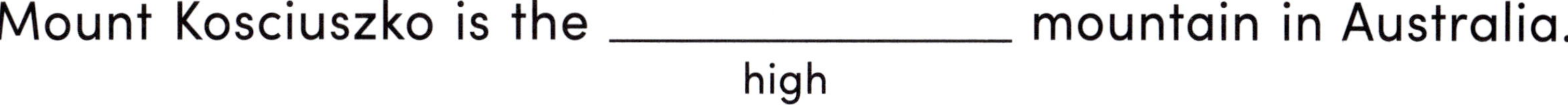

Unit 15

Say Listen Look Understand Remember Practise	
most	______
post	______
piano	______
radio	______
hope	______
rose	______
joke	______
woke	______
broke	______
quote	______
My own words	
______	______
______	______
______	______

1 Circle the pictures with a **long o** sound.

2 Write the words.

j, w, p, ch, br → oke

______
______
______
______
______

m, p → ost

______
______

3 Write a list word.

______

______

Spelling Rules! Student Book 1 (ISBN 9780655092582) © Janelle Ho, Helen Pearson/Matilda Education Australia

4 Write the joke you like the most. Draw a picture to match.

____

____

____

____

____

____

____

Rule Words with a silent **e** drop the **e** before adding **ed** or **ing**.

5 Colour the correct word.

My aunt | posted | posting | my present today.

I am | hoping | hopeing | it will arrive tomorrow.

Mr Kumar | poseed | posed | some questions to his class.

Mum is always | quoteing | quoting | Grandma.

6 Use the clue to write a list word.

Something funny ______________

To say what someone else said ______________

Past tense of wake ______________

Reflection

- I can do this.
- I am not sure.
- I need help.

Unit 16

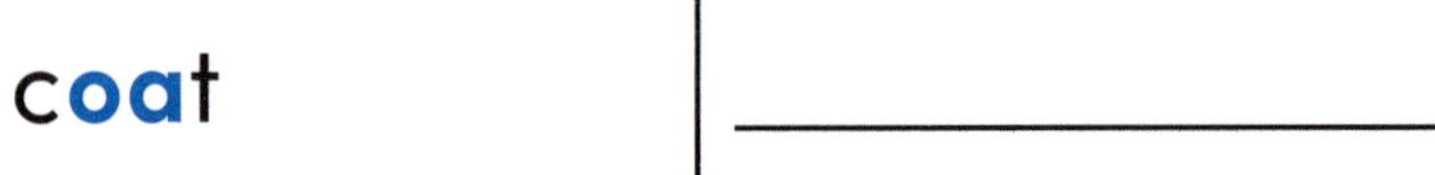

Say Listen Look Understand Remember Practise	
coat	___
goat	___
soap	___
loaf	___
float	___
toast	___
show	___
flow	___
know	___
yellow	___
My own words	
___	___
___	___
___	___

1 Write a list word.

___

___

___

Can you write the word for this picture?

___

2 Write **oa** or **ow**.

sh__ __ l__ __f

kn__ __ fl__ __t

yell__ __ t__ __st

3 Make new words.

gl, sl, bl → ow
___
___
___

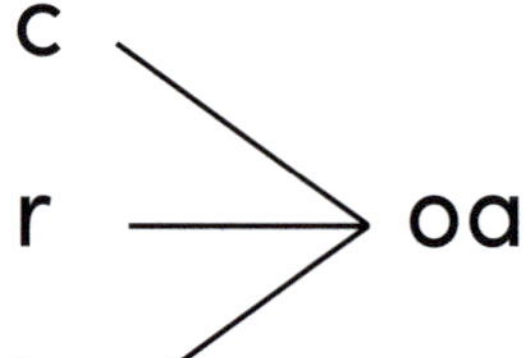

c, r, b → oast
___
___
___

Spelling Rules! Student Book 1 (ISBN 9780655092582) © Janelle Ho, Helen Pearson/Matilda Education Australia

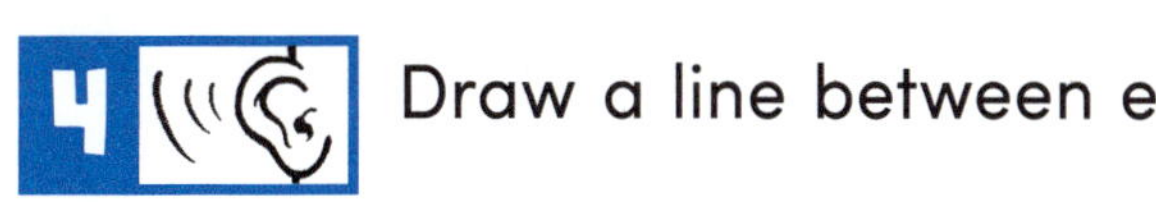

Draw a line between each sound.

loaf	float	toast	soap
flow	show	know	yellow

Which word has a silent letter? ____________

Use the clues to complete the puzzle.

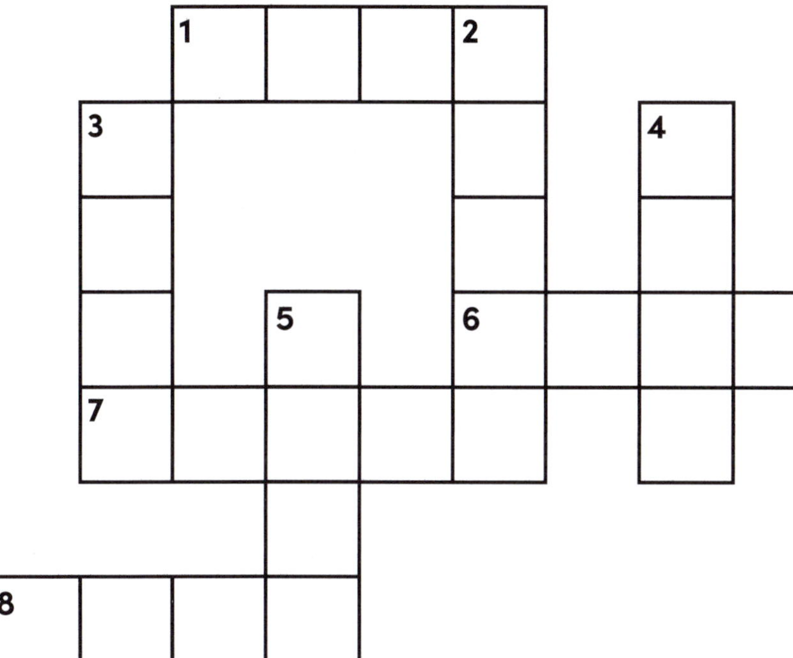

1. Row, row, row your _____ .
2. cheese on _____
3. a _____ of bread
4. wear this to keep warm
5. something funny
6. wash your hands with _____
7. lie on water
8. dogs like to chew one

6 The words **road**, **rowed** and **rode** are homophones. Colour the correct homophone.

Joan | road | rode | rowed | a pony and I | road | rode | rowed | a boat.

Why did the chicken cross the | road | rode | rowed |?

Spelling Rules! Student Book 1 (ISBN 9780655092582) © Janelle Ho, Helen Pearson/Matilda Education Australia

Unit 17

Say Listen Look Understand Remember Practise	
beach	______
teach	______
speech	______
bunch	______
lunch	______
flash	______
crash	______
crush	______
blush	______
swish	______
My own words	
______	______
______	______
______	______

1 Say the list words. Sort the words by their vowel sound.

same as see
______
______
______

same as fun
______
______
______
______

same as bat
______
______

same as tin
______

2 Follow the pattern to make new words.

bunch	crash	crash	beach
m_ _ _ _	cl_ _ _	_ _ ush	p_ _ _ _
cr_ _ _ _	spl_ _ _	_ _ unch	r_ _ _ _

Spelling Rules! Student Book 1 (ISBN 9780655092582) © Janelle Ho, Helen Pearson/Matilda Education Australia

Add **es** to words that end in **ch** or **sh**.

Plural: *beaches* *lunches* *flashes*

Present tense: *teaches* *munches* *wishes*

 Colour the correct word.

Alan | mashs | mashes | a banana before adding it to the batter.

Su-Ing | swishs | swishes | the water around in her mouth.

My dog | munches | munchs | and | crunches | crunchs | his bone so loudly!

 Add **s** or **es**.

pull___ and push___

munch___ and crunch___

teach___ and learn___

wash___ and wipe___

crash___ and bash___

lunch___ and dinner___

 Draw a picture to match the sentence.

Max made a big splash at the beach.

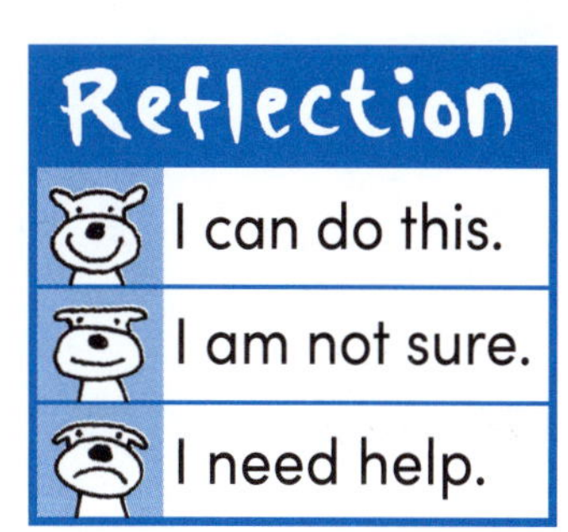

Spelling Rules! Student Book 1 (ISBN 9780655092582) © Janelle Ho, Helen Pearson/Matilda Education Australia

Unit 18

Say Listen Look Understand Remember Practise	
shout	______
about	______
around	______
house	______
pounce	______
town	______
crowd	______
brown	______
flower	______
allow	______
My own words	
______	______
______	______
______	______

1 Make **ou** words.

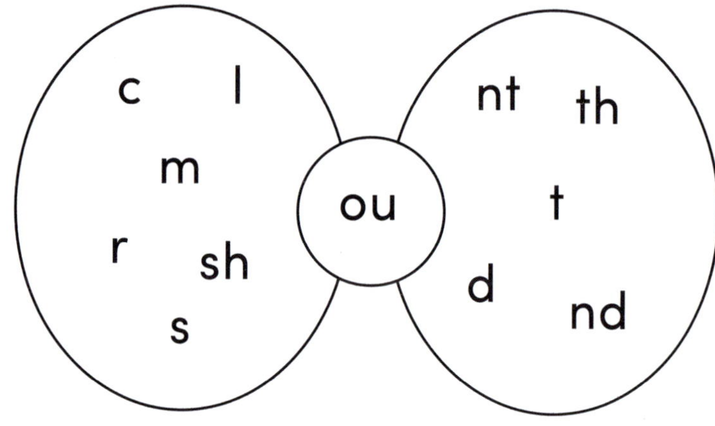

______

______

______

2 Write these words as two syllables.

about = ___ + ______

around = ___ + ______

aloud = ___ + ______

3 Use the clues to make **ow** words.

~~t~~ → d

______

~~n~~ → d

______

~~fl~~ → sh

______

4 Write a list word that rhymes.

ground crown mouse power loud

______ ______ ______ ______ ______

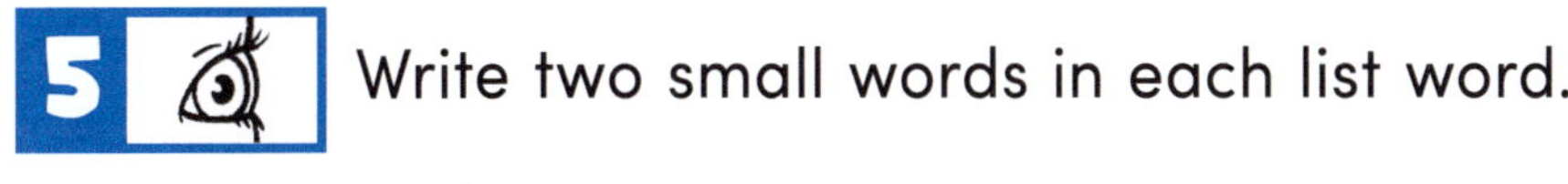

5 Write two small words in each list word.

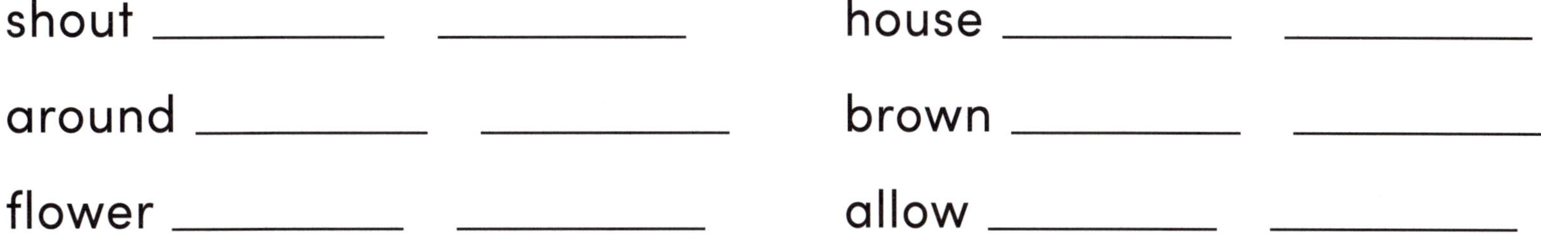

shout ______ ______ house ______ ______

around ______ ______ brown ______ ______

flower ______ ______ allow ______ ______

6 Write the plural.

one two h__ __ se__ one two m__ __ th__

one two cl__ __ d__ one two cl__ __ n__

one two fr__ __ n__ one two fl__ __ er__

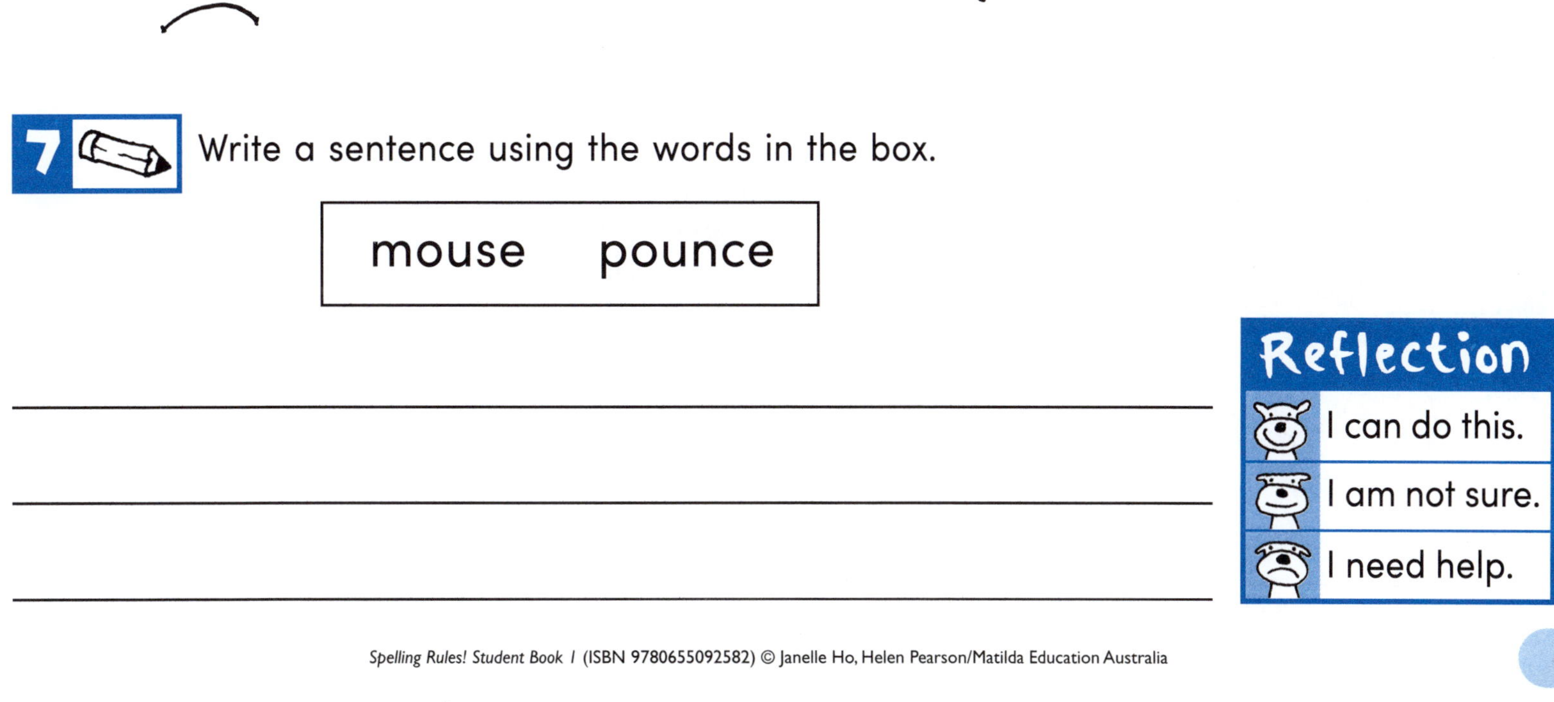

7 Write a sentence using the words in the box.

mouse	pounce

____

____

____

Reflection

I can do this.

I am not sure.

I need help.

Unit 19

Do you want this toy?

Say Listen Look Understand Remember Practise	
toy	
enjoy	
annoy	
loyal	
coin	
noise	
oil	
spoil	
point	
toilet	
My own words	

1 Draw the shapes for the words.

toy

oil

spoil

enjoy

point

annoy

loyal

2 Write the list word that matches the face.

____________ ____________

3  Add **ed**.

enjoy ____________

spoil ____________

point ____________

Spelling Rules! Student Book 1 (ISBN 9780655092582) © Janelle Ho, Helen Pearson/Matilda Education Australia

oy sounds the same as **oi**.
A syllable with **oi** must always end in a consonant.

joy *join* *boy* *boil*

Fill in **oy** or **oi** to show the vowel sound.

b__ __	s__ __l	j__ __nt	n__ __se	c__ __l
c__ __	ann__ __	sp__ __l	enj__ __	t__ __let

Change one letter to make a list word.

joint	ail	soy	royal	coil
________	________	________	________	________

Write a rhyming word to finish each sentence.

My favourite salad dressing is vinegar and ____________.
boil

Quick! Eat the peaches or they will ____________.
toil

Can you ____________ me in the right direction?
joint

Our cat loves to ____________ our dog.
joy

Spelling Rules! Student Book 1 (ISBN 9780655092582) © Janelle Ho, Helen Pearson/Matilda Education Australia

Unit 20

Say Listen Look Understand Remember Practise	
who	____________
why	____________
when	____________
where	____________
what	____________
which	____________
wheel	____________
whale	____________
white	____________
wheat	____________
My own words	
____________	____________
____________	____________
____________	____________

1 Find a small word in the list word. Write the small word.

when ____________ ____________

what ____________ ____________

wheel ____________ ____________ ____________

where ____________ ____________ ____________

wheat ____________ ____________ ____________

white ____________ ____________

2 Write the words.

w — ish ____________
w — ent ____________
w — ind ____________

wh — eel ____________
wh — ite ____________
wh — ale ____________

Spelling Rules! Student Book 1 (ISBN 9780655092582) © Janelle Ho, Helen Pearson/Matilda Education Australia

 Choose the correct word for each riddle.

why	where	what	when	which

_ _ _ did the boy take a ruler to bed?

To see how long he slept.

_ _ _ _ can a net hold water?

When the water is ice.

_ _ _ _ can run but not walk?

Your nose.

_ _ _ _ _ do frogs keep their money?

In river banks.

_ _ _ _ _ pet only lives on the floor?

A carpet.

These words are easy to mix up.

were = past tense of are

we're = we are

where = indicates a place

 Write **Were**, **We're** or **Where**.

____________ you going out?

____________ are you going?

____________ going to the library.

Reflection

- I can do this.
- I am not sure.
- I need help.

Spelling Rules! Student Book 1 (ISBN 9780655092582) © Janelle Ho, Helen Pearson/Matilda Education Australia

1 Write **ou**, **oa** or **ow** words in the correct balloon.

makes the sound in br**ow**n

ou words	**ow** words
____________	____________
____________	____________
____________	____________
____________	____________

makes the sound in yell**ow**

oa words	**ow** words
____________	____________
____________	____________
____________	____________
____________	____________

2 Add **s** or **es** to make a plural.

one rose, two ____________

one coin, two ____________

one bunch, two ____________

one soap, two ____________

one wheel, two ____________

one speech, two ____________

one crash, two ____________

3 Add **ed**.

joke ____________

toast ____________

enjoy ____________

allow ____________

pounce ____________

blush ____________

crowd ____________

Spelling Rules! Student Book 1 (ISBN 9780655092582) © Janelle Ho, Helen Pearson/Matilda Education Australia

4 Change **y** to **i** before adding **es** or **ed**.

spy + es ____________ cry + es ____________ dry + es ____________

spy + ed ____________ cry + ed ____________ dry + ed ____________

5 Circle the wrong word in each sentence. Write the word correctly on the line.

When the water boyls, make a cup of tea. ____________

I don't know wat to eat for lunch. ____________

Some pieces of cruched ice floated in my drink. ____________

My dog loves to run arround the block. ____________

The flowers where picked by my neighbour. ____________

6 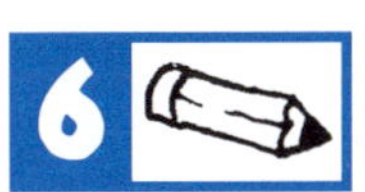 Write a word that fits the clue.

have a good time ____________

a piece of cooked bread ____________

copy what someone says ____________

a form of money ____________

7  Some words have more than one meaning.
Write two different meanings for each word.

right 1 ______________________________

2 ______________________________

spoil 1 ______________________________

2 ______________________________

Unit 22

What a big splash!

Say Listen Look Understand Remember Practise	
splash	____________
split	____________
spray	____________
sprain	____________
sprint	____________
street	____________
stripe	____________
screen	____________
scream	____________
scrub	____________
My own words	
____________	____________
____________	____________
____________	____________

1 Circle in green the words beginning with **st**. Circle in blue the words beginning with **str**.

2 Write the missing consonants.

s __ __ ash

__ __ ray

__ c __ eam

s __ __ atch

3 Write the list word that has the small word in it.

lit	rain	ripe	rub
____________	____________	____________	____________

Spelling Rules! Student Book 1 (ISBN 9780655092582) © Janelle Ho, Helen Pearson/Matilda Education Australia

 Use the vowel sounds to group the list words.

sounds like **feel**

____
____
____

sounds like **make**

____
____

sounds like **fit**

____
____

sounds like **but**

____

sounds like **cat**

____

sounds like **side**

____

Rule

If a word has a short vowel, followed by a single consonant, double the consonant before adding **ed** or **ing**.

spot	*spotted*	*spotting*
plan	*planned*	*planning*

5 Add **ed** or **ing**.

	scrub	strap	strum
Add **ed**	______________	______________	______________
Add **ing**	______________	______________	______________

6 Write a sentence about the street where you live.

____
____
____

Reflection

- I can do this.
- I am not sure.
- I need help.

Unit 23

One, two, three.

Say Listen Look Understand Remember Practise	
three	
throat	
thread	
throw	
throne	
thrill	
shrill	
shrub	
shrug	
shriek	
My own words	

1 Write list words.

2 Circle the word in each column that has a different vowel sound.

thrill	throat	three
shrill	strong	thread
spite	throne	shriek

Spelling Rules! Student Book 1 (ISBN 9780655092582) © Janelle Ho, Helen Pearson/Matilda Education Australia

 Use the clues to make list words.

th + ______ th + ______

thr + ______ shr + ______

sh +  ______ sh + 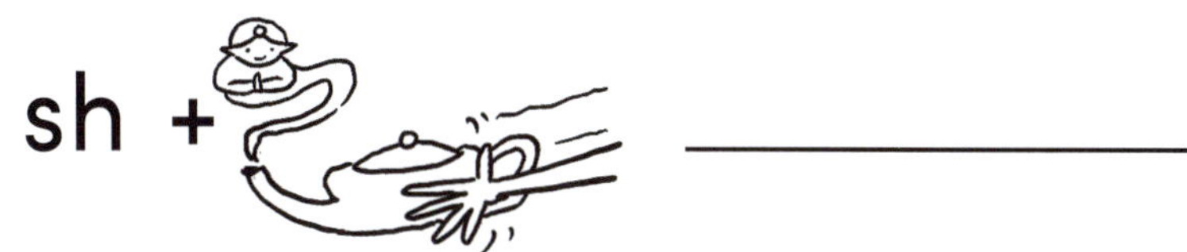 ______

 Write these sentences again with a space between each word.

Mythroatfeelsverydry. ____________________

Canyoueatthreeeggs? ____________________

Theridewasfullofthrills. ____________________

5 Draw a line between each sound.

three	throw	throne	thrill
shrub	shrug	shriek	shrink

 Circle the correct word.

Our class was | thrilld | thrilled | to meet an Aboriginal elder.

There are trees and | shrubs | shrubbs | in our garden.

Tai | shruged | shrugged | to show he did not mind.

I | shrieked | shriekked | when I saw the rat.

Reflection

- I can do this.
- I am not sure.
- I need help.

Spelling Rules! Student Book 1 (ISBN 9780655092582) © Janelle Ho, Helen Pearson/Matilda Education Australia

Unit 24

You stink!

Thank you.

Say Listen Look Understand Remember Practise	
fling	
spring	
angry	
hungry	
finger	
sink	
plank	
shrink	
ankle	
blanket	
My own words	

1 Find a list word for each clue. What is the hidden word under the star?

1. joint above your foot
2. throw
3. after winter, before summer
4. something to keep you warm
5. wash up here

2 Two list words have been combined into one. Write the list words.

plankle ______ ______

flinger ______ ______

Spelling Rules! Student Book 1 (ISBN 9780655092582) © Janelle Ho, Helen Pearson/Matilda Education Australia

3 Make words. Write the words to match the clues.

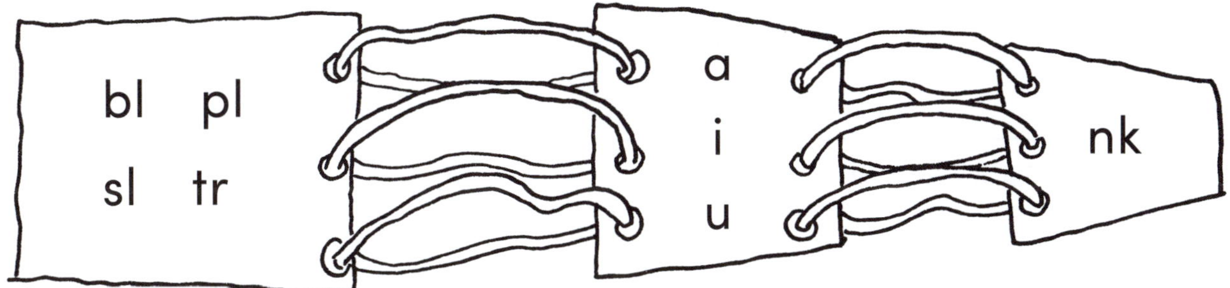

_ _ _ _ _   _ _ _ _ _   _ _ _ _ _   _ _ _ _ _

empty	piece of wood	creep	elephant's nose

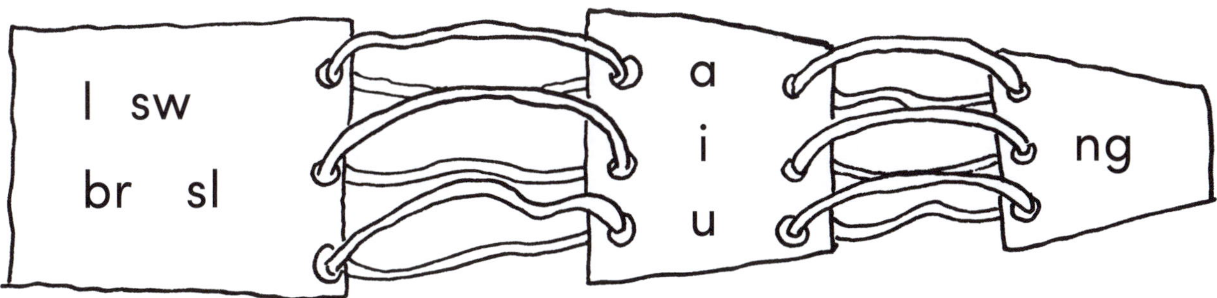

_ _ _ _   _ _ _ _ _   _ _ _ _ _   _ _ _ _ _

a body organ	move back and forth	informal language	carry

Most words add **ed** to show the past tense but some words change. These words are called **irregular verbs**.

sing → sang

4 Write the past tense by following the pattern.

sink	spring	shrink
s _ nk	spr _ _ _	_ _ _ _ _ _

- I can do this.
- I am not sure.
- I need help.

Unit 25

Say Listen Look Understand Remember Practise	
boo	___
roof	___
cool	___
smooth	___
choose	___
balloon	___
cartoon	___
bedroom	___
bathroom	___
boomerang	___
My own words	
___	___
___	___
___	___

1 Say the words. If **oo** makes the sound in t**oo**k, colour the picture red. If **oo** makes the sound in f**oo**d, colour the picture yellow.

2 Draw a line between each sound. Underline each syllable. Write the number of syllables in the circle.

smooth ◯ cartoon ◯ balloon ◯

choose ◯ bathroom ◯ boomerang ◯

Spelling Rules! Student Book 1 (ISBN 9780655092582) © Janelle Ho, Helen Pearson/Matilda Education Australia

When two words join together to make a new word, it is called a **compound word**.
Football is a compound word.

3 Write the names of these rooms. Write two more compound words of your own.

bed
bath → room
class

____
____
____

[ ] [ ]

Proofread the story. There are six mistakes. Circle the mistakes. Write the words correctly at the end.

It is dark and cold. Dad and I sit on the roof to lock at the moon. I have warm botts on. We have food. It is cak and ice-cream. Clang! I drop my spon. It falls off the roof and into the pooll. Splash! It is gon.

______________ ______________
______________ ______________
______________ ______________

Reflection
- I can do this.
- I am not sure.
- I need help.

Unit 26

Say Listen Look Understand Remember Practise	
new	______
few	______
dew	______
news	______
knew	______
drew	______
threw	______
screw	______
jewel	______
view	______
My own words	
______	______
______	______
______	______

1 Say each list word. Sort the words by their sound.

sounds like new

______

______

______

______

______

sounds like drew

______

______

______

2 Write the list words that match each clue.

a word that has a silent letter ______

two words that are homophones ______ ______

a word that has two syllables ______

Spelling Rules! Student Book 1 (ISBN 9780655092582) © Janelle Ho, Helen Pearson/Matilda Education Australia

These words are **irregular verbs**.
They do not add **ed** to show the past tense.

draw → drew *know → knew*
grow → grew *throw → threw*

 Write the past tense for these irregular verbs.

draw ________ know ________ throw ________ grow ________

 Write the past tense for these regular verbs.

screw ________ view ________ scream ________ cool ________

 Circle the correct word.

I gave some books away so now I have | few | fewer |.

Many | jewels | jewells | in the necklace glittered.

The desks in the classroom are | new | news | knew |.

Can you please | throw | threw | the ball to me?

6 Make compound words.

news + paper ____________________

dew + drop ____________________

screw + driver ____________________

Unit 27

Say Listen Look Understand Remember Practise	
cute	
tune	
tube	
refuse	
true	
glue	
clue	
argue	
value	
rescue	
My own words	

1 Say each list word. Sort the words by their sound.

sounds like new

sounds like drew

2 Write a list word to match the clue.

not ugly ______

melody ______

not false ______

stick together ______

say no ______

disagree ______

Spelling Rules! Student Book 1 (ISBN 9780655092582)

3 Use the clues to write new words.

~~g~~ → c

glue ______________________

use this to help get the answer

~~c~~ → b

____

mix yellow and this to get green

4 Write the word when the silent **e** is removed.

cute __________ tube __________

Rule

Words with a silent **e** drop the **e** before adding **ed**, **ing**, **er** or **est**.

tune	*tuned*	*tuning*
cute	*cuter*	*cutest*

5 Add the correct suffix.

Stop ________________ ! You are giving me a headache.
argue

I like this colour best. It is the ________________ one.
blue

The fireman ________________ my cat from the tree.
rescue

6 Add a letter to make a list word. You may need to rearrange the letters.

nut ______________ reuse ______________ vale ______________

Reflection

I can do this.

I am not sure.

I need help.

Unit
28
Revision

 Say the word. Write the consonants to complete the word.

 _ _ _ing

 fi_ _er

 _ _ _atch

 _ _ _ill

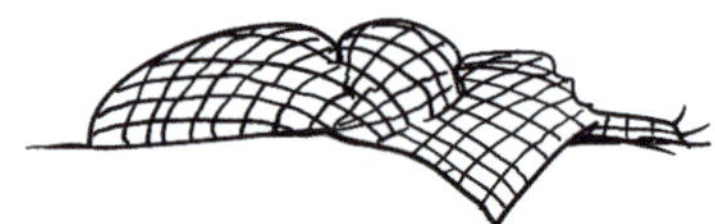 bla_ _et

 _ _ _iek

 Write **oo**, **u-e**, **ue** or **ew**.

f_ _d	tr_ _	n_ _s	t_n_
cart_ _n	arg_ _	ch_ _	ref_s_
br_ _m	bl_ _	dr_ _	J_n_

 Add letters to build a new word.

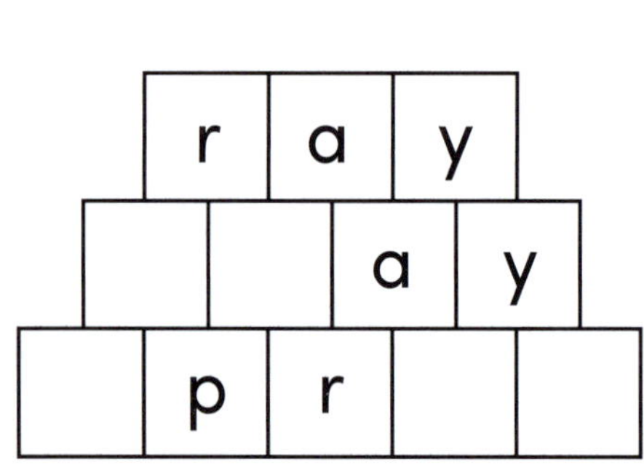

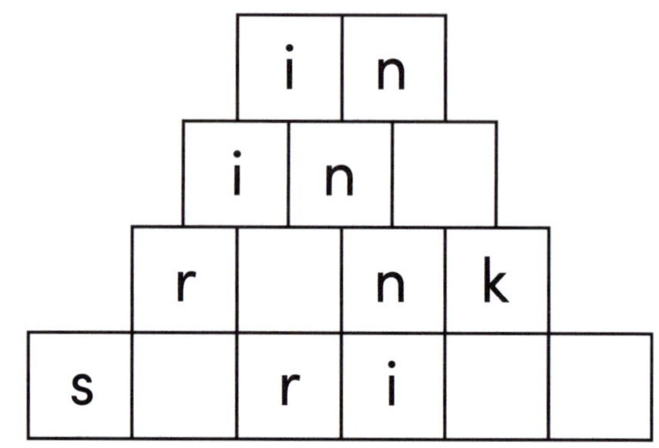

4 Write a word to match the picture clue.

Aboriginal Australians use a 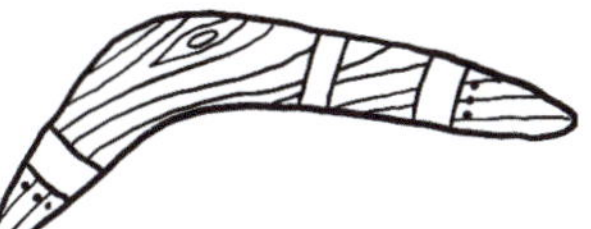 ________________ to hunt.

________________ is an important food for Aboriginal Australians.

5 Write the past tense. Use your spelling rules. Remember that some words do not add **ed**.

scream	________________	cool	________________
view	________________	rescue	________________
argue	________________	shrug	________________
scrub	________________	throw	________________
grow	________________		

flew is the past tense of ________________

6 Circle nouns in green. Colour verbs in yellow. Underline adjectives in red. Some words might belong to more than one group.

stripe	throne	new	choose
ankle	spring	rescue	angry

7 Use the beginning of the first word and the end of the second word to make a third word.

spring + hint = ________________ three + shrill = ________________

shy + grub = ________________ hunt + angry = ________________

small + tooth = ________________ split + winter = ________________

Unit 29

Say Listen Look Understand Remember Practise	
one	____________
two	____________
three	____________
four	____________
five	____________
six	____________
seven	____________
eight	____________
nine	____________
ten	____________
My own words	
____________	____________
____________	____________
____________	____________

1 Write the numbers in the rhyme.

__________, __________,

buckle my shoe.

__________, __________,

knock at the door.

__________, __________,

pick up sticks.

__________, __________,

lay them straight.

__________, __________,

a big fat hen!

Cluck

Pop

2 Write the number that rhymes. Remember that the spelling may be different!

door	__________	tree	__________	bun	__________
ticks	__________	gate	__________	men	__________
shoe	__________	hive	__________	line	__________

Spelling Rules! Student Book 1 (ISBN 9780655092582) © Janelle Ho, Helen Pearson/Matilda Education Australia

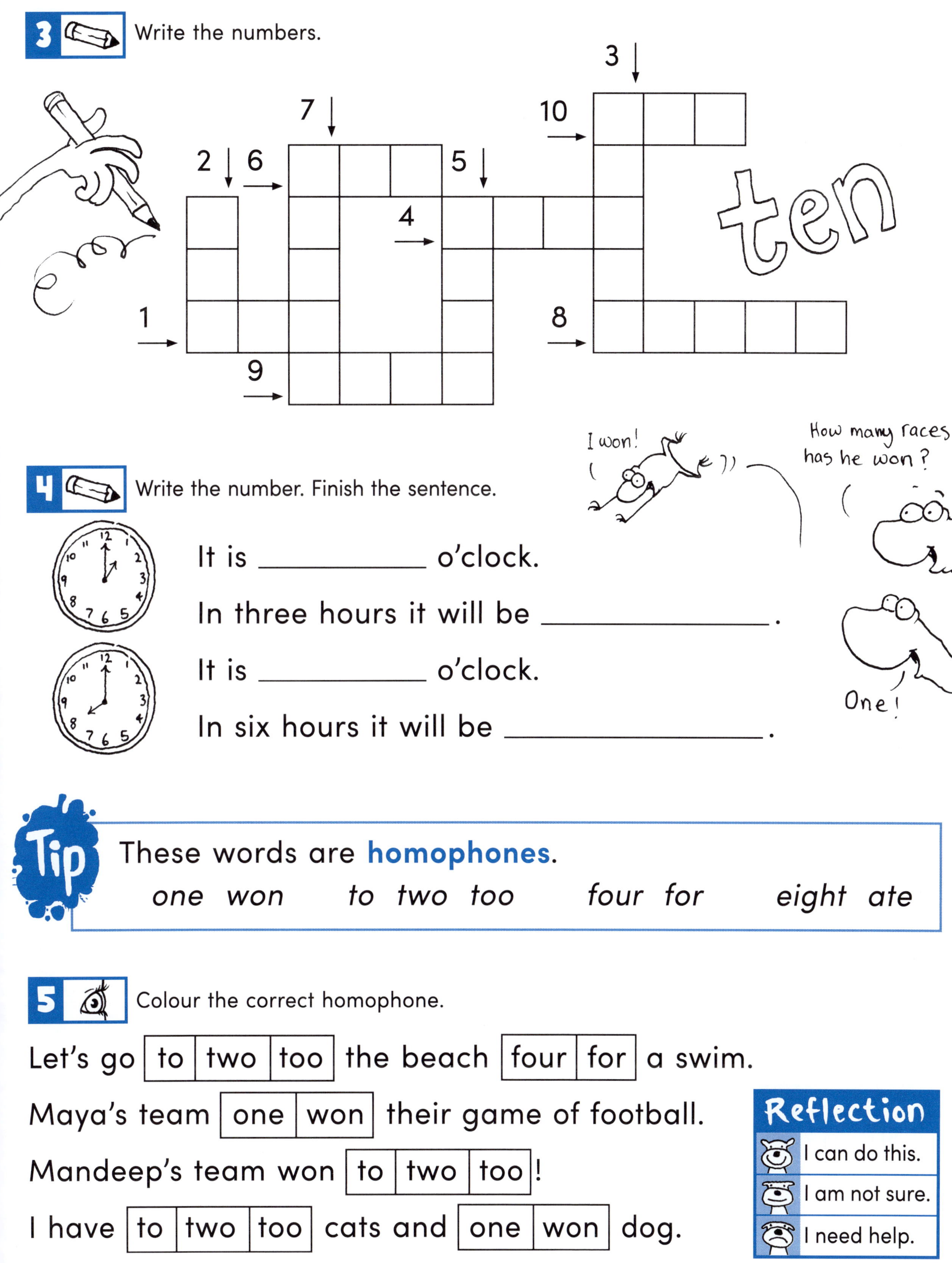

3 Write the numbers.

1 →, 2 ↓, 3 ↓, 4 →, 5 ↓, 6 →, 7 ↓, 8 →, 9 →, 10 →

4 Write the number. Finish the sentence.

It is ____________ o'clock.

In three hours it will be ________________.

It is ____________ o'clock.

In six hours it will be ________________.

Tip

These words are **homophones**.

one won *to two too* *four for* *eight ate*

5 Colour the correct homophone.

Let's go | to | two | too | the beach | four | for | a swim.

Maya's team | one | won | their game of football.

Mandeep's team won | to | two | too |!

I have | to | two | too | cats and | one | won | dog.

Reflection

I can do this.

I am not sure.

I need help.

Unit 30

Say Listen Look Understand Remember Practise	
bull	______
pull	______
push	______
put	______
sugar	______
look	______
cook	______
wood	______
stood	______
shook	______
My own words	
______	______
______	______
______	______

1 Write **u** or **oo**.

Little Bo Peep has lost her sheep. Where can she l_ _k?

P_t a little s_gar in Mum's tea.

2 Use the letters to make **ook** words. Write the word again.

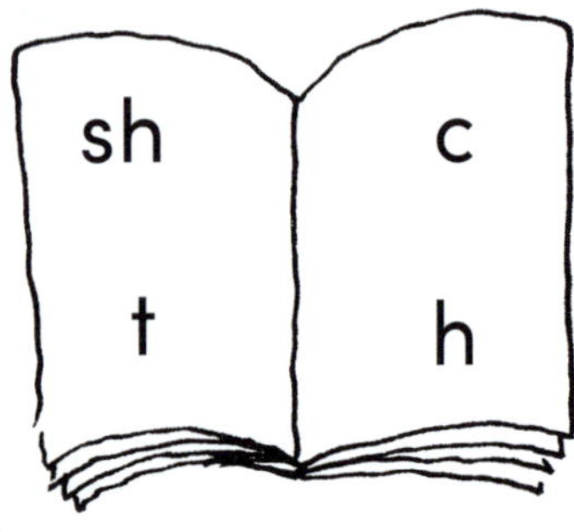

_ook ______ _ook ______

_ook ______ _ _ook ______

3 Draw the shape for each word.

bull　　　look　　　push

4 Write two list words for each shape.

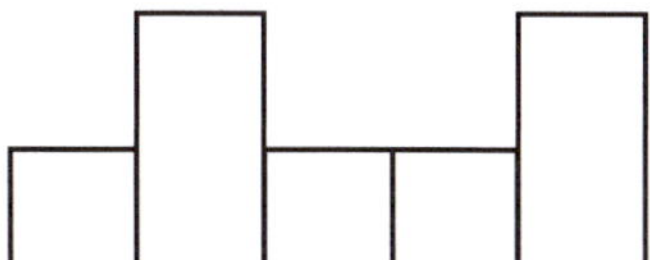

5 One word in each row has a different vowel sound. Circle the word.

put	pull	cut	foot
room	book	drew	glue

6 The past tense of these words are list words. Write the list words.

stand ______________　　　shake ______________

7 Write sentences using the words.

look ____

____

cook ____

____

Spelling Rules! Student Book 1 (ISBN 9780655092582) © Janelle Ho, Helen Pearson/Matilda Education Australia

Unit 31

Say Listen Look Understand Remember Practise	
held	___
bald	___
hold	___
scold	___
world	___
build	___
could	___
would	___
should	___
shoulder	___
My own words	
___	___
___	___
___	___

1 Write six old words.

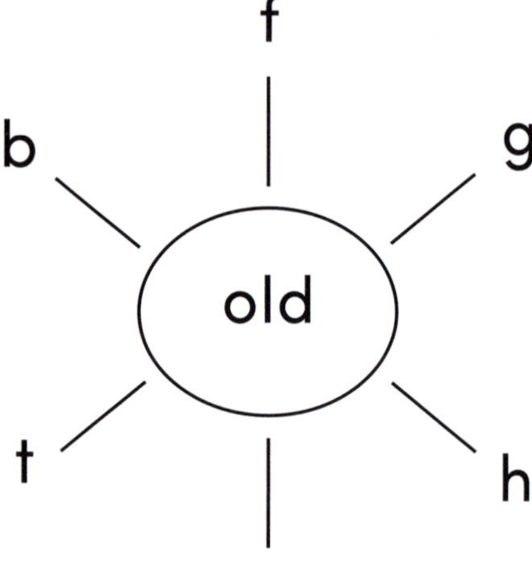

___ ___
___ ___
___ ___

c
sh — ould — w

___ ___
___

2 Say both words. Colour the correct one.

A | bald | bold | man has no hair.

Can you | held | hold | my bag, please?

This is the house that Jack | build | built |.

Spelling Rules! Student Book 1 (ISBN 9780655092582) © Janelle Ho, Helen Pearson/Matilda Education Australia

3 Write the plural.

bull ______ world ______ cook ______ shoulder ______

Wood and *would* are **homophones**.

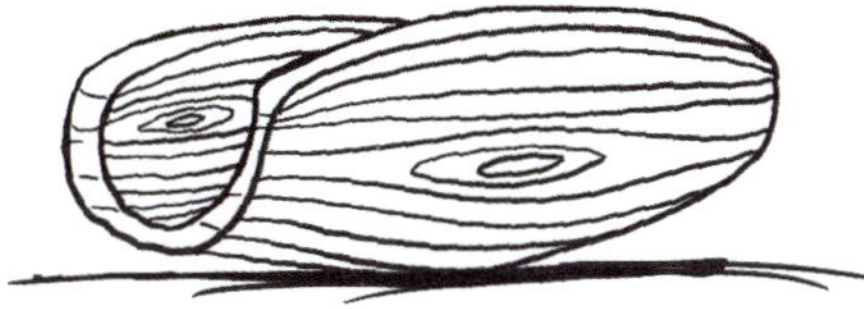

4 Circle the correct word.

Jaya [wood | would] like to make something nice from the [piece | peace] of [wood | would].

5 Write the correct word.

could would should

6 Write all the words you can see in the word worm.

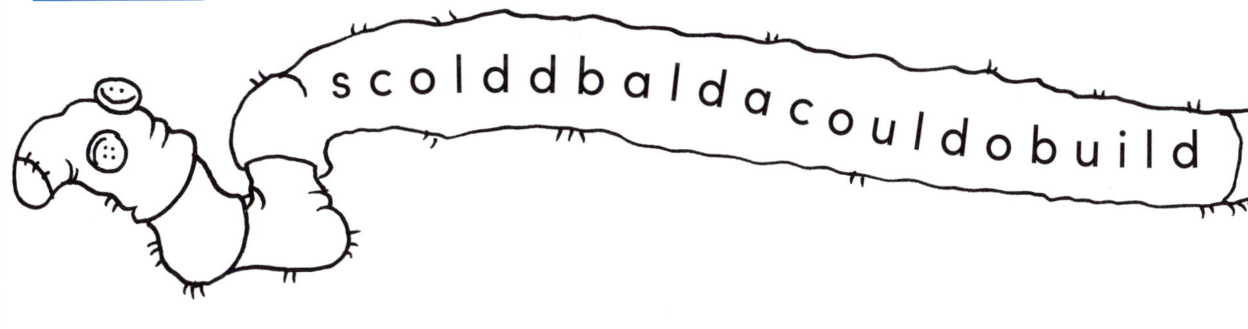

____

Unit 32

Say Listen Look Understand Remember Practise	
sunhat	________
gumboot	________
bedside	________
shoelace	________
toenail	________
jellyfish	________
earring	________
hairbrush	________
newspaper	________
wheelchair	________
My own words	
________	________
________	________
________	________

1  Join the pictures to make a compound word. Write the word.

____

 + 

____

 + 

____

 + 

____

Compound words are made up of two words.

bed + room = bedroom *shoe + lace = shoelace*

2  Draw a line to show the two words in each compound word.

bedside toenail newspaper earring

Spelling Rules! Student Book 1 (ISBN 9780655092582) © Janelle Ho, Helen Pearson/Matilda Education Australia

Write compound words.

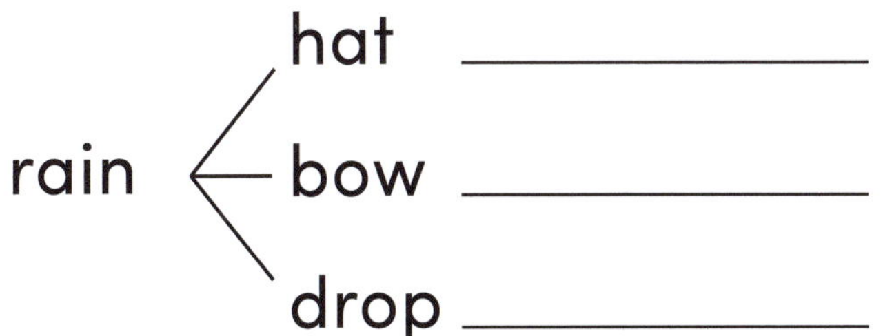

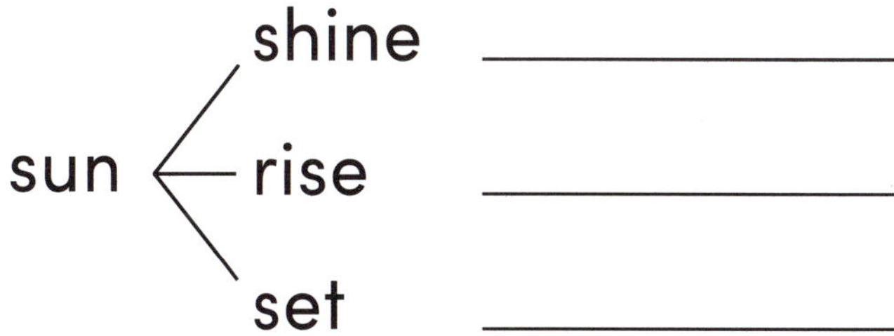

Draw a line to match the words and make compound words. Each compound word is a body part.

arm jaw finger ear rib belly

button pit cage bone nail lobe

Write the things you see in the bedroom. Draw more items that are compound words. Write these words too.

Unit 33

Say Listen Look Understand Remember Practise	
mother	______
father	______
sister	______
brother	______
grandmother	______
grandfather	______
elder	______
aunt	______
uncle	______
family	______
My own words	
______	______
______	______
______	______

1 Look at each family. Fill in the missing words.

Kim Helen Nick Tim Sam

Helen is Sam's ______.

Nick is his ______.

Tim is his ______.

Kim is his ______.

Helen will have a ______ soon.

Then there will be six people in Sam's ______.

Ling Lee

Lee has no br ______ or si______.

Ling is her ______.

Tareq Reem Yusef

______ is Yusef's ______.

______ is his ______.

Spelling Rules! Student Book 1 (ISBN 9780655092582) © Janelle Ho, Helen Pearson/Matilda Education Australia

 Circle the picture if you can hear **er** at the end.

 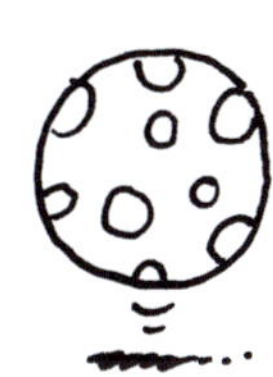   

 Who are the members of your family? Draw a family tree.

 Write the meaning of each word.

elder ______________________________

grandmother ______________________________

grandfather ______________________________

aunt ______________________________

uncle ______________________________

 Add the ending to the word. Write the new word.

small + er ____________ big + er ____________

What does the **er** ending do?

____

Reflection

 I can do this.

 I am not sure.

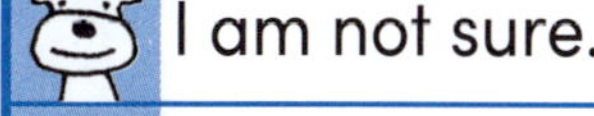 I need help.

Unit 34

Say Listen Look Understand Remember Practise	
baker	___
writer	___
driver	___
swimmer	___
manager	___
builder	___
actor	___
doctor	___
sailor	___
author	___
My own words	
___	___
___	___
___	___

Tip er or or at the end of a word often names a job.

1 Draw a line to match the word with the picture.

actor

sailor

doctor

teacher

Rule If a word ends in silent e, drop the silent e before adding er. *bake → baker* *drive → driver*

If a word has a short vowel followed by one consonant, double the consonant before adding er.

run → runner *swim → swimmer*

Spelling Rules! Student Book 1 (ISBN 9780655092582) © Janelle Ho, Helen Pearson/Matilda Education Australia

2 Write the list word.

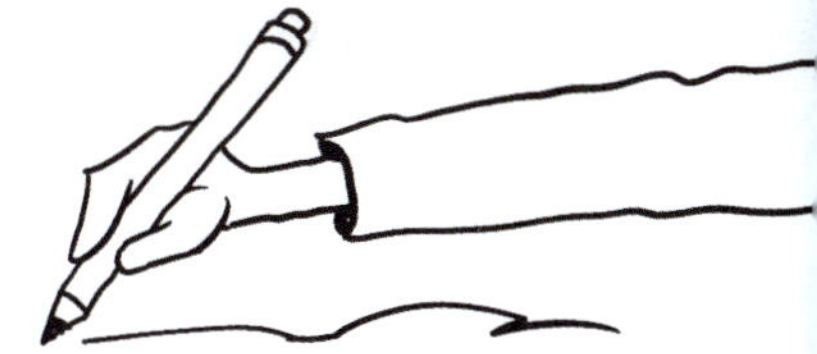

Write all the list words where the silent **e** was dropped.

____

Write all the list words where the final consonant was doubled.

____

Write all the list words where there was no change.

____

Write the two words left. ____________ ____________

3 Write a list word to complete each sentence.

I look after the sick. I am not a nurse. I am a ____________.

I bake bread and rolls. I am a ____________.

I work on a ship. I am a ____________.

I write books. I am an ____________.

I work in the theatre and on television. I am an ____________.

I build homes and offices. I am a ____________.

4 Add **er** or **or** to make names of jobs. Remember the spelling rules.

paint	____________	edit	____________
rule	____________	inspect	____________
babysit	____________	garden	____________

Reflection

- I can do this.
- I am not sure.
- I need help.

Unit 35 Revision

 Follow the vowel pattern to write two words with the same vowel sound.

boom	look	put	drew
___ oo ___	___ oo ___	___ u ___	_____ ew
________	________	________	________

 Circle the word in each row that has a different vowel sound.

would	could	should	shoulder
flow	show	allow	yellow
go	who	most	post
lie	chief	piece	shield

 What is my family doing? Write words that end in **er**.

I am sitting on the step.

My __________ sits at the computer.

My __________ cooks lunch.

My __________ reads a book.

My __________ is fast asleep.

I will see my grandmother tomorrow. She is an __________ and will teach me how to care for Country.

Spelling Rules! Student Book 1 (ISBN 9780655092582) © Janelle Ho, Helen Pearson/Matilda Education Australia

4 Write compound words.

bath — room ____________
bath — tub ____________
bath — robe ____________

bed — side ____________
sea — side ____________
road — side ____________

5 Add **er** or **est**. Remember your spelling rules.

	high	stale	funny
Add **er**	____________	____________	____________
Add **est**	____________	____________	____________

6 **er** or **or** have been added to a base word. Write the base word.

actor	writer	robber	manager
____________	____________	____________	____________

7 Write the past tense of the word. Remember your spelling rules. Watch out for irregular verbs!

The wind ____________ the leaves off the tree.
blow

Russ ____________ three kilograms lighter than last year!
weigh

Lila ____________ an opening in her chess game and
spot

____________ her piece to win.
move

List words in unit order

Unit 1
hip
hop
ship
shop
dish
fill
shell
pack
wish
luck

Unit 2
clap
crab
flag
glad
plot
stop
skin
trip
crack
smell

Unit 3
fast
chest
desk
wasp
hint
grunt
stamp
spilt
crust
grand

Unit 4
baby
potato
save
face
blame
shame
stale
break
great
steak

Unit 5
brain
plain
chain
sail
trail
again
pay
stay
sway
away

Unit 6
they
grey
prey
obey
eight
weigh
weight
sleigh
neigh
neighbour

Unit 8
tall
small
dull
stiff
cliff
stuff
bluff
grass
dress
buzz

Unit 9
equal
even
week
keep
sleep
east
steal
speak
dream
cheat

Unit 10
chief
thief
field
shield
piece
believe
key
honey
monkey
turkey

Unit 11
jelly
silly
happy
body
puppy
funny
sunny
bumpy
sleepy
wobbly

Unit 12
kind
lion
tiger
behind
five
nine
glide
try
spy
reply

Unit 13
pie
lie
tie
sigh
high
thigh
right
night
bright
flight

Unit 15
most
post
piano
radio
hope
rose
joke
woke
broke
quote

Unit 16
coat
goat
soap
loaf
float
toast
show
flow
know
yellow

Unit 17
beach
teach
speech
bunch
lunch
flash
crash
crush
blush
swish

Spelling Rules! Student Book 1 (ISBN 9780655092582) © Janelle Ho, Helen Pearson/Matilda Education Australia

Unit 18
shout
about
around
house
pounce
town
crowd
brown
flower
allow

Unit 19
toy
enjoy
annoy
loyal
coin
noise
oil
spoil
point
toilet

Unit 20
who
why
when
where
what
which
wheel
whale
white
wheat

Unit 22
splash
split
spray
sprain
sprint
street
stripe
screen
scream
scrub

Unit 23
three
throat
thread
throw
throne
thrill
shrill
shrub
shrug
shriek

Unit 24
fling
spring
angry
hungry
finger
sink
plank
shrink
ankle
blanket

Unit 25
boo
roof
cool
smooth
choose
balloon
cartoon
bedroom
bathroom
boomerang

Unit 26
new
few
dew
news
knew
drew
threw
screw
jewel
view

Unit 27
cute
tune
tube
refuse
true
glue
clue
argue
value
rescue

Unit 29
one
two
three
four
five
six
seven
eight
nine
ten

Unit 30
bull
pull
push
put
sugar
look
cook
wood
stood
shook

Unit 31
held
bald
hold
scold
world
build
could
would
should
shoulder

Unit 32
sunhat
gumboot
bedside
shoelace
toenail
jellyfish
earring
hairbrush
newspaper
wheelchair

Unit 33
mother
father
sister
brother
grandmother
grandfather
elder
aunt
uncle
family

Unit 34
baker
writer
driver
swimmer
manager
builder
actor
doctor
sailor
author

LIST WORDS IN ALPHABETICAL ORDER

about	Unit 18
actor	Unit 34
again	Unit 5
allow	Unit 18
angry	Unit 24
ankle	Unit 24
annoy	Unit 19
argue	Unit 27
around	Unit 18
aunt	Unit 33
author	Unit 34
away	Unit 5
baby	Unit 4
baker	Unit 34
bald	Unit 31
balloon	Unit 25
bathroom	Unit 25
beach	Unit 17
bedroom	Unit 25
bedside	Unit 32
behind	Unit 12
believe	Unit 10
blame	Unit 4
blanket	Unit 24
bluff	Unit 8
blush	Unit 17
body	Unit 11
boo	Unit 25
boomerang	Unit 25
brain	Unit 5
break	Unit 4
bright	Unit 13
broke	Unit 15
brother	Unit 33
brown	Unit 18
build	Unit 31
builder	Unit 34
bull	Unit 30
bumpy	Unit 11
bunch	Unit 17
buzz	Unit 8
cartoon	Unit 25
chain	Unit 5
cheat	Unit 9
chest	Unit 3
chief	Unit 10
choose	Unit 25
clap	Unit 2
cliff	Unit 8
clue	Unit 27
coat	Unit 16
coin	Unit 19
cook	Unit 30
cool	Unit 25
could	Unit 31
crab	Unit 2
crack	Unit 2
crash	Unit 17
crowd	Unit 18
crush	Unit 17
crust	Unit 3
cute	Unit 27
desk	Unit 3
dew	Unit 26
dish	Unit 1
doctor	Unit 34
dream	Unit 9
dress	Unit 8
drew	Unit 26
driver	Unit 34
dull	Unit 8
earring	Unit 32
east	Unit 9
eight	Unit 6
elder	Unit 33
enjoy	Unit 19
equal	Unit 9
even	Unit 9
face	Unit 4
family	Unit 33
father	Unit 33
fast	Unit 3
few	Unit 26
field	Unit 10
fill	Unit 1
finger	Unit 24
five	Unit 12
flag	Unit 2
flash	Unit 17
flight	Unit 13
fling	Unit 24
float	Unit 16
flow	Unit 16
flower	Unit 18
four	Unit 29
funny	Unit 11
glad	Unit 2
glide	Unit 12
glue	Unit 27
goat	Unit 16
grand	Unit 3
grandfather	Unit 33
grandmother	Unit 33
grass	Unit 8
great	Unit 4
grey	Unit 6
grunt	Unit 3
gumboot	Unit 32
hairbrush	Unit 32
happy	Unit 11
held	Unit 31
high	Unit 13
hint	Unit 3
hip	Unit 1
hold	Unit 31
honey	Unit 10
hop	Unit 1
hope	Unit 15
house	Unit 18
hungry	Unit 24
jelly	Unit 11
jellyfish	Unit 32
jewel	Unit 26
joke	Unit 15
keep	Unit 9
key	Unit 10
kind	Unit 12
knew	Unit 26
know	Unit 16
lie	Unit 13
lion	Unit 12
loaf	Unit 16
look	Unit 30
loyal	Unit 19
luck	Unit 1
lunch	Unit 17
manager	Unit 34
monkey	Unit 10
most	Unit 15
mother	Unit 33
neigh	Unit 6
neighbour	Unit 6
new	Unit 26
news	Unit 26
newspaper	Unit 32
night	Unit 13
nine	Unit 12
noise	Unit 19

obey Unit 6
oil Unit 19
one Unit 29

pack Unit 1
pay Unit 5
piano Unit 15
pie Unit 13
piece Unit 10
plain Unit 5
plank Unit 24
plot Unit 2
point Unit 19
post Unit 15
potato Unit 4
pounce Unit 18
prey Unit 6
pull Unit 30
puppy Unit 11
push Unit 30
put Unit 30

quote Unit 15

radio Unit 15
refuse Unit 27
reply Unit 12
rescue Unit 27
right Unit 13
roof Unit 25
rose Unit 15

sail Unit 5
sailor Unit 34
save Unit 4
scold Unit 31
scream Unit 22
screen Unit 22
screw Unit 26
scrub Unit 22
seven Unit 29
shame Unit 4
shell Unit 1
shield Unit 10
ship Unit 1
shoelace Unit 32
shook Unit 30
shop Unit 1
should Unit 31
shoulder Unit 31
shout Unit 18
show Unit 16
shriek Unit 23
shrill Unit 23
shrink Unit 24
shrub Unit 23
shrug Unit 23
sigh Unit 13
silly Unit 11
sink Unit 24
sister Unit 33
six Unit 29
skin Unit 2
sleep Unit 9
sleepy Unit 11
sleigh Unit 6
small Unit 8
smell Unit 2
smooth Unit 25
soap Unit 16
speak Unit 9
speech Unit 17
spilt Unit 3
splash Unit 22
split Unit 22
spoil Unit 19
sprain Unit 22
spring Unit 24
sprint Unit 22
spray Unit 22
spy Unit 12
stale Unit 4
stamp Unit 3
stay Unit 5
steak Unit 4
steal Unit 9
stiff Unit 8
stood Unit 30
stop Unit 2
street Unit 22
stripe Unit 22
stuff Unit 8
sugar Unit 30
sunhat Unit 32
sunny Unit 11
sway Unit 5
swimmer Unit 34
swish Unit 17

tall Unit 8
teach Unit 17
ten Unit 29
they Unit 6
thief Unit 10
thigh Unit 13
thread Unit 23
three Unit 23
threw Unit 26
thrill Unit 23
throat Unit 23
throne Unit 23
throw Unit 23
tie Unit 13
tiger Unit 12
toast Unit 16
toenail Unit 32
toilet Unit 19
town Unit 18
toy Unit 19
trail Unit 5
trip Unit 2
true Unit 27
try Unit 12
tube Unit 27
tune Unit 27
turkey Unit 10
two Unit 29

uncle Unit 33

value Unit 27
view Unit 26

wasp Unit 3
week Unit 9
weigh Unit 6
weight Unit 6
whale Unit 20
what Unit 20
wheat Unit 20
wheel Unit 20
wheelchair Unit 32
when Unit 20
where Unit 20
which Unit 20
white Unit 20
who Unit 20
why Unit 20
wish Unit 1
wobbly Unit 11
woke Unit 15
wood Unit 30
world Unit 31
would Unit 31
writer Unit 34

yellow Unit 16

SPELLING RULES AND TIPS

- A **syllable** makes one beat in a word.
  A syllable has a vowel sound in it.
  mum = 1 syllable *mother* = 2 *grandmother* = 3

- Most words add **s** to show there is more than one. *chip→chips*
  Some words change. *man→men* *child→children*
  Some words stay the same. *sheep* *deer* *fish*
  Words that end in **ch** or **sh** add **es**. *beach→beaches* *flash→flashes*

- You can add **y** to some words to make an adjective. *sleep→sleepy*
  If a word has a short vowel sound, double the last letter before adding **y**. *sun→sunny*

- You can add **s**, **es**, **ed**, **ing**, **er** or **est** to many words.
  If a word ends in silent **e**, drop the **e** before adding **ed**, **ing**, **er** or **est**.
  bake→baked *bake→baking* *bake→baker*
  cute→cuter *cute→cutest*
  If a word has a short vowel sound, double the last letter before adding **ed**, **ing**, **er** or **est**.
  slip→slipped *slip→slipping* *swim→swimmer*
  fit→fitter *fit→fittest*
  If a word ends in **y**, change **y** to **i**, before adding **es**, **ed**, **er** or **est**.
  cry→cries *cry→cried*
  happy→happier *happy→happiest*
  Some verbs do not add **ed** to show the past tense. They are called **irregular verbs**.
  sing→sang *sink→sank* *draw→drew* *grow→grew*

- When two words are joined together to make a new word, it is called a **compound word**. *sun + hat→sunhat*

- Words that sound the same but are not spelt the same are called **homophones**.
  sale/sail *week/weak* *piece/peace* *wood/would*

- Some words have letters you cannot hear. ***k**now* ***k**nee* ***k**night*

Spelling Rules! Student Book 1 (ISBN 9780655092582) © Janelle Ho, Helen Pearson/Matilda Education Australia